Prayer

Conversation with the Almighty

Prayer
Conversation with the Almighty

Vinu V Das

TP

Tabor Press

ISBN 978-1-997541-10-3

Table of Contents

Chapter 1: The Essence of Prayer

1.1 Definition and Nature of Prayer

1.1.1 Communicating with God

Prayer, at its most basic level, is an act of communication between human beings and God. Unlike ordinary interpersonal communication, however, prayer is both transcendent and deeply personal—it engages the human spirit and is directed to the Divine Creator (Psalm 19:14). This is no mere exchange of words; it is a form of communion that can involve praise, petition, confession, thanksgiving, or the simple outpouring of emotion. To say that prayer is "communicating with God" suggests that both speaking and listening are integral to this exchange. While many people focus primarily on their own words—requests, pleas, expressions of gratitude—prayer also includes being still and receptive to God's presence, nudges, or insights (Psalm 46:10).

In Scripture, the earliest depictions of prayer show how foundational it is for God's people. In the opening chapters of Genesis, individuals such as Adam and Eve experience direct communication with God in the Garden of Eden (Genesis 3:8). Though the term "prayer" is not explicitly used in these verses, the relational exchange between the Creator and the first humans is implicit in the text. Later, we see more explicit references to people "calling upon the name of the Lord" (Genesis 4:26), indicating that communication with God became a pattern for worship and seeking help. From these early snapshots of biblical history onward, believers have recognized that prayer stands at the core of a God-centered life. It is the means by which humans invite God into every facet of their existence—personal, communal, emotional, and spiritual.

Moreover, prayer is not limited to formal settings or religious institutions. While there are occasions in Scripture where prayers occur in the tabernacle or the temple (e.g., 1 Kings 8:22–53), we also see individuals praying in their homes, in the wilderness, in prisons, and on journeys. This universality underscores prayer's essence as communication accessible to all people, regardless of location or social status (James 5:13–14). Thus, the first dimension of the definition of prayer is that it involves an ongoing dialogue with a God who is both transcendent (beyond all creation) and immanent (near to each believer). The biblical record testifies that God welcomes this dialogue and responds in ways that demonstrate His loving character and sovereign plan.

1.1.2 The Heart Attitude in Prayer

While the act of speaking or thinking words directed to God is certainly central to prayer, the Bible repeatedly emphasizes that the posture of the heart is even more crucial. For example, King David, recognized for his profound intimacy with God, prayed in Psalm 51:17 that "a broken and contrite heart, O God, you will not despise." This statement reveals an important truth: prayer is not simply about the right formula of words, but about an honest, humble approach toward the Almighty. Words that spring from genuine reverence, dependence, and love reflect a heart that truly seeks God.

In stark contrast, Scripture also depicts the wrong kind of heart attitude in prayer. Jesus criticizes the Pharisees who made a show of their long prayers in public (Matthew 6:5). Even though they were praying outwardly, their underlying motive was self-glorification. This highlights that the essence of prayer goes beyond external expressions or ritualized formulas; rather, it is rooted in sincerity, faith, and humility (Luke 18:9–14). The parable of the tax collector and the Pharisee underscores how God values the authenticity and remorse of a penitent heart over the self-assured boasting of a religious figure.

A related theme in Scripture is that faith is a foundational condition for true prayer (Hebrews 11:6). Whether one is asking for divine intervention, offering praise, or simply resting in God's presence, faith opens the door to deeper communion. Faith in prayer acknowledges that God both hears and has the power to respond according to His will. This does not mean one should expect every supplication to be answered in a straightforward or predetermined manner; rather, it means trusting that God is sovereign, loving, and able to work beyond human limitations. By maintaining this attitude of faith, believers position themselves to experience an authentic relationship with the Creator in prayer.

In essence, the heart attitude in prayer is one of humility, sincerity, and trust. It stands in opposition to pride, hypocrisy, or manipulative intentions. For believers, this fosters spiritual maturity as they grow more dependent on God, acknowledging their need for His guidance, forgiveness, and sustaining grace. This posture of the heart not only shapes the effectiveness of prayer but also transforms the individual who prays, molding them more and more into the likeness of Christ.

1.2 Biblical Foundations

1.2.1 Old Testament Concepts of Communion with God

In the Old Testament, prayer develops against the backdrop of Israel's unfolding history with God. Though the earliest patriarchs, such as Abraham, Isaac, and Jacob, did not always follow a formal system or liturgy, they practiced a form of prayer that included both verbal and silent communication with God. Abraham, for instance, famously interceded for the city of Sodom (Genesis 18:22–33), demonstrating an interactive, almost conversational approach. This anecdote reveals that prayer involves reasoning and pleading with God based on His character—namely, His justice and mercy. Abraham's approach underscores that the essence of prayer includes seeking alignment with God's righteousness and compassion.

Likewise, the story of Hannah in 1 Samuel 1:10–13 offers a poignant example of heartfelt prayer in the Old Testament context. She pours out her grief before the Lord, silently moving her lips but speaking from the depth of her anguish. Her prayer is intensely personal, yet it lays bare a universal theme: genuine communion with God can be raw, unvarnished, and vulnerable. In fact, the priest Eli initially mistakes Hannah for a drunken woman because of her silent yet fervent prayer posture. This confusion serves to highlight how prayer is sometimes misunderstood when judged solely by outward appearance; its true meaning is rooted in the condition of one's heart and the authenticity of one's cry to God.

The use of psalms in Israel's worship also points to the Old Testament foundation of prayer. The Book of Psalms functions as both the hymnbook and the prayerbook of ancient Israel. While many psalms are communal, there are also deeply personal psalms of lament, thanksgiving, and praise (Psalm 13, Psalm 23, Psalm 100, etc.). These prayers demonstrate that communication with God embraces the full range of human emotion and experience. The psalmists do not shy away from questions, doubts, despair, or joy; rather, they turn every facet of their emotional life into an occasion for communion with God (Psalm 42:1–5). By doing so, they model a holistic approach to prayer, suggesting that a believer need not mask their troubles or confusions but can bring them openly before the Lord.

Additionally, the Old Testament context shows that prayer was intrinsically linked with sacrifice and worship in the Tabernacle and later in the Temple (2 Chronicles 6:12–42). This integration underscores the reverence and ritual purity associated with approaching God. Yet, even with these structural elements, the underlying principle of sincere devotion remains paramount. The prophets frequently rebuke the Israelites for offering sacrifices and prayers with insincere hearts (Isaiah 1:11–15). Once again, it becomes clear that no outward form can replace the genuine inner devotion God seeks. Thus, from the Old Testament vantage point, prayer is far more than a ritual or performance; it is a sacred meeting between finite humanity and an infinite, holy God.

1.2.2 New Testament Emphasis on Intimacy and Relationship

In the New Testament, the essence of prayer receives its fullest expression through the life and teachings of Jesus Christ. Jesus not only taught His disciples to pray (Matthew 6:9–13) but also modeled a prayer-saturated life. Whether retreating to lonely places to pray (Luke 5:16) or praying publicly before significant events (John 11:41–42), Jesus demonstrated that prayer is the lifeblood of an intimate relationship with the Father. This intimate communion is a defining feature of the New Testament perspective: believers are invited to call God "Abba, Father" (Romans 8:15; Mark 14:36), indicating a warmth and closeness that was far more explicit than many of the images seen in the Old Testament.

Moreover, the apostolic writings build upon Jesus's example, stressing the indwelling presence of the Holy Spirit. The Holy Spirit assists believers in prayer, especially in moments of weakness or uncertainty (Romans 8:26–27). This reflects a Trinitarian dimension to prayer: Christians pray to the Father, in the name of the Son, and by the power of the Holy Spirit (Ephesians 2:18). Such a framework underscores the deeply relational nature of prayer in the New Testament. Far from being a one-way monologue, prayer becomes a participation in the divine life, as believers are drawn into fellowship with God through the agency of the Spirit.

Additionally, the New Testament clarifies that prayer forms an indispensable part of the believer's continuous relationship with God. References like 1 Thessalonians 5:17 ("pray without ceasing") and Colossians 4:2 ("continue steadfastly in prayer") encourage an ongoing conversation that transcends formal moments of petition. This does not necessarily mean believers should neglect set times of prayer, but rather that their entire life is lived in communion with God, ready to turn to Him at any moment. The emphasis here is on a living, dynamic relationship that shapes the believer's character, decisions, and perspective.

Crucially, the New Testament also affirms that the sincere heart remains central to prayer. Jesus points out the folly of mere repetition or empty phrases, instructing His followers not to pray like the pagans who think they will be heard because of "many words" (Matthew 6:7). Instead, He invites them to approach the Father confidently, rooted in the knowledge of God's goodness and faithfulness. This perspective, emphasized throughout the Gospels and Epistles, cements the truth that prayer is meant to be a heartfelt, honest dialogue with a loving God, rather than a formulaic ritual.

1.3 Purpose of Prayer

1.3.1 Glorifying God

One of the foundational purposes of prayer in the Bible is to glorify God. Glorifying God involves recognizing His supreme worth, honoring His attributes, and exalting His name above every other concern. Indeed, biblical prayers often begin or end with expressions of praise that magnify God's holiness, power, mercy, and love. This is clearly seen in many of the Psalms, which open with praise before delving into the psalmist's petitions or confessions (Psalm 100:4–5). Even the well-known Lord's Prayer commences with the words, "Our Father in heaven, hallowed be your name" (Matthew 6:9), placing the focus immediately on God's sanctity and honor.

When believers pray with the intention of glorifying God, they align their hearts with the ultimate reality that creation exists for the praise of its Maker. Such a perspective prevents prayer from devolving into a purely self-serving exercise, reminding those who pray that they are coming before the King of kings. This humility not only brings spiritual growth but also fosters an attitude of reverence. In Exodus 15:1–2, for example, Moses and the Israelites break into song after crossing the Red Sea. Their prayerful outburst of praise glorifies God by recounting His mighty acts and upholding His name as worthy of eternal acclaim.

Furthermore, glorifying God through prayer can also manifest in thanksgiving. When believers thank God for blessings received, for His sustaining grace, or for the wonders of salvation, they acknowledge that every good gift is ultimately from Him (James 1:17). This gratitude-centered approach is particularly powerful because it shifts attention away from personal anxieties and onto the faithfulness of God. Even in difficult circumstances, scriptural prayers show that believers can still find reasons to glorify God, trusting that His purposes are higher than human comprehension (Habakkuk 3:17–19).

Finally, glorifying God in prayer reinforces the communal nature of the faith. In passages like Acts 4:24–31, the early church lifts a united prayer that begins with acknowledging God as the sovereign Creator. Their corporate worship centers on God's majesty before they present their requests for boldness in preaching the Gospel. By setting God's glory as the primary aim, the church ensures that their unity is anchored in a shared recognition of who God is and what He has done.

1.3.2 Seeking Divine Guidance

Alongside glorifying God, seeking divine guidance stands as one of the foremost reasons believers turn to prayer. Throughout the biblical narrative, people frequently bring their uncertainties, decisions, and dilemmas to God, trusting that He will provide direction in due time. For instance, Joshua 9:14 implies a subtle rebuke when the Israelites fail to "ask counsel from the Lord" before making a treaty with the Gibeonites, underscoring the importance of consulting God in significant matters. Conversely, in 2 Samuel 2:1, David inquires of the Lord regarding whether he should go up to one of the cities of Judah, setting an example of how prayer can guide believers in everyday, as well as momentous, decisions.

Seeking divine guidance is not an attempt to manipulate God into approving one's own preferences. Rather, it is an act of submission, acknowledging that God's wisdom surpasses human understanding (Proverbs 3:5–6). In practice, this often involves an honest surrender of personal agendas, asking for insight into God's perspective and will. While the answer may not always come in an audible voice or dramatic revelation, Scripture affirms that God delights in guiding His people, especially when they approach Him with genuine humility. James 1:5 promises that if anyone lacks wisdom, they should ask God, who gives generously without reproach. This underscores both the generosity of God and His willingness to guide those who earnestly seek His counsel.

Guidance in prayer also intersects with discernment in moral and spiritual issues. Believers often face ethical questions or dilemmas, and turning to prayer invites God's transformative presence to clarify what is right and good in a given situation (Philippians 1:9–10). In this way, prayer is not merely about receiving strategic direction—where to go, what to do—but also about growing in an understanding of God's character, which shapes the believer's worldview and ethical conduct. When Scripture and prayer come together, believers develop a well-rounded sense of divine guidance, informed by both the written Word of God and the prompting of the Holy Spirit (Psalm 119:105; John 14:26).

Moreover, seeking divine guidance is not merely an individual pursuit; it can be a communal endeavor. In Acts 13:1–3, the leaders of the church in Antioch fasted and prayed together, seeking the Holy Spirit's leading for mission work. As a result, they were directed to set apart Paul and Barnabas for the work to which God had called them. This story exemplifies how prayer for guidance can unite believers in purpose and action, illustrating that discerning God's will can happen within the context of a praying community.

1.4 Extended Reflections on the Essence of Prayer

Since *The Essence of Prayer* serves as the foundational chapter of this book, it bears reiterating that everything in prayer forms a cohesive whole.

1. **Prayer as Communion, Not Performance**: Throughout the Old and New Testaments, the aim of prayer is intimate communion with God rather than performance. Time and again, Scripture warns against the temptation to "pray for show," echoing Jesus's criticism of the Pharisees (Matthew 6:5). When we reduce prayer to a performance aimed at impressing others, we undermine the essence of genuine communion. Instead, biblical prayer points to a quiet, honest conversation with God in the secret place of one's

heart (Matthew 6:6). Here, the Lord sees what is done in secret and rewards authenticity, not eloquence.

2. **Prayer's Relationship to Covenant**: From an Old Testament standpoint, prayer is deeply intertwined with the concept of covenant. Israel's relationship with God was framed by covenant obligations and blessings (Exodus 24:3–8). Prayers of repentance, petition, and thanksgiving are all covenantal in nature, reflecting Israel's status as God's chosen people. By praying, Israelites acknowledged their dependence on God and renewed their commitment to live according to His statutes. This reliance becomes a testament to how prayer constantly reaffirms and embodies the covenant bond, reinforcing loyalty and reminding the faithful of God's promises. While the term "covenant" might sound legalistic, it actually underscores the relational aspects at the heart of prayer—God and His people are bound together by divine love and faithfulness.

3. **Emotional Range in Prayer**: One of the most powerful aspects of prayer in the Bible is its capacity to encompass the full spectrum of human emotion. From the exultant praises of Miriam (Exodus 15:20–21) to the bitter laments of Jeremiah (Jeremiah 20:7–18), Scripture validates the expression of joy, sorrow, confusion, fear, gratitude, anger, and more within the context of prayer. This emotional honesty highlights that prayer is not about being polite or presenting a sanitized version of oneself. Instead, it is about authenticity before a God who sees every facet of the human heart (Psalm 139:1–4). By bringing real emotions to God, believers lay hold of divine comfort, correction, and transformation.

4. **Holiness of God and the Fear of the Lord**: Scripture consistently portrays God as utterly holy. Recognizing

God's holiness is central to understanding the essence of prayer because it calls believers to approach God with reverential awe (Isaiah 6:3–5). This "fear of the Lord" does not imply cowering dread but rather a deep respect that acknowledges God's infinite purity and power. It fosters humility and a sense of wonder, essential attitudes in genuine prayer. Even though believers are invited to draw near with confidence (Hebrews 4:16), they do so with the recognition that they stand before the King of Glory. This mixture of boldness and reverence underlines the privilege of prayer while also guarding against frivolity.

5. **Prayer as a Lifelong Journey**: The Bible depicts individuals who engage in prayer over the course of their entire lives, learning through both successes and failures. Jacob wrestles with God (Genesis 32:24–30), Elijah prays in times of national crisis (1 Kings 18:36–39), and Daniel maintains a steadfast rhythm of prayer even under the threat of persecution (Daniel 6:10). Their experiences suggest that prayer is not a static or singular event but an ongoing journey of faith. Over time, these biblical figures come to know God more intimately, trust Him more deeply, and reflect His character more fully. The same is true for believers today: prayer shapes and is shaped by the journey of faith, forging a deeper bond between the believer and the Creator.

6. **Synergy Between Prayer and Scripture**: Prayer in the Bible is never divorced from God's revealed Word. Indeed, many prayers recorded in Scripture draw directly from God's promises or recall His mighty deeds. Nehemiah's prayer (Nehemiah 1:5–11), for example, begins with a recitation of God's covenant faithfulness and addresses Israel's sin in light of divine commands. This shows that prayer is most

powerful when it is grounded in God's truth—Scripture informs believers about who God is, what He has done, and what He has promised. As people pray the truths of Scripture, they align their hearts with God's own revealed will. This synergy produces a vibrant and effective prayer life that is both anchored in biblical reality and responsive to personal and communal needs.

7. **Transformational Aspect of Prayer**: Another key dimension of the essence of prayer is transformation. Romans 12:2 exhorts believers to be transformed by the renewing of their minds. Prayer is part of this process, as it places the believer in God's presence, where they can be changed to reflect Christ's character. The very act of praying fosters dependence on God, reshaping one's outlook on trials, blessings, relationships, and responsibilities. In prayer, fear can be replaced by courage, resentment by forgiveness, and despair by hope. This transformation is not merely incidental; it is central to the purpose of prayer. By drawing near to God in prayer, believers open themselves to the work of the Holy Spirit, who refines their faith and molds their desires to align with God's.

8. **Faith as the Crucible of Prayer**: Faith weaves itself through every dimension of biblical prayer. Whether seen in the petitions of a desperate father seeking healing for his child (Mark 9:24) or the unwavering trust of a martyr in the face of death, faith is the catalyst that propels the believer into prayer. It is also the means by which prayers are sustained when no immediate answer is evident. This is especially relevant in moments of uncertainty or suffering, where faith compels believers to keep seeking God's presence. Faith acknowledges that God is near, that He cares, and

that He is capable of intervening. Such reliance may be tested by trials, but it also grows stronger through persistent prayer. Indeed, James 1:2–4 suggests that the testing of faith produces perseverance, which in turn matures the believer.

9. **Community Dimension**: While personal prayer remains vital, biblical narratives also underscore the communal aspect of prayer (2 Chronicles 7:14; Acts 2:42). The early church, for example, was "devoted to the apostles' teaching and the fellowship, to the breaking of bread and the prayers" (Acts 2:42). These corporate gatherings of prayer carried immense power, uniting believers in a shared vision of God's greatness and in collective requests for His guidance or intervention. Community prayer can foster unity, empathy, and shared accountability, ensuring that prayer is not solely a private affair. Even so, the essence remains the same: heartfelt communication with God, whether as individuals or as a collective body of believers.

10. **Dependence and Surrender**: Ultimately, the essence of prayer boils down to dependence on God and surrender to His will. Jesus's own prayer in the Garden of Gethsemane (Luke 22:41–42) stands as a supreme example: "Father, if you are willing, remove this cup from me. Nevertheless, not my will, but yours, be done." Here, we see Jesus entrusting His deepest agony to the Father's plan. This points to the most profound dimension of prayer's essence: it invites believers into a relationship where their will is brought into alignment with God's purposes, even when that alignment requires self-denial or the acceptance of suffering. In so doing, prayer becomes not just a means of receiving blessings, but a school of discipleship where believers learn

to echo Christ's submission, "Your will be done."

1.5 Integrating the Essence of Prayer into Daily Faith

To conclude this first chapter, it is helpful to reflect on how the essence of prayer—its definition as communication with God, the importance of heart attitude, biblical foundations, and its purposes—integrates into daily faith. While subsequent chapters will discuss the more practical aspects (how to pray, when to pray, examples of who prayed, etc.), a few key points here can anchor one's understanding:

- **Cultivating an Awareness of God's Presence**: Since prayer is rooted in communion with a relational God, believers benefit from regularly reminding themselves that God is present and accessible. This awareness turns everyday moments into opportunities for prayerful conversation—whether offering silent thanks, seeking a quick word of wisdom, or simply acknowledging the Lord's companionship in ordinary tasks.

- **Guarding the Heart**: Recognizing the heart's posture as paramount helps believers remain vigilant against the temptations of pride, hypocrisy, or mere routine. Periodic self-examination—asking whether one's prayers are motivated by a desire to glorify God or by self-interest—can maintain a purity of intention.

- **Embracing the Tension Between Boldness and Reverence**: Prayer invites both childlike boldness (Hebrews 4:16) and humble awe (Isaiah 6:3–5). Holding these two attitudes together guards against the extremes of casual irreverence and paralyzing fear. Instead, believers approach God with confidence in His love and humility in His holiness.

- **Anchoring Prayer in Scripture**: Since the Bible is God's primary revelation, grounding one's prayers in scriptural truths enriches communion with God and ensures that believers align their supplications with biblical wisdom. Whether through praying specific psalms or meditating on promises found in the Gospels and Epistles, Scripture-infused prayer fosters spiritual depth.

- **Trusting God's Character in All Circumstances**: Prayer is most transformative when it is rooted in trust. Even when answers tarry or circumstances seem bleak, believers can cling to the knowledge that God is good, faithful, and sovereign. Holding fast to these truths in prayer cultivates resilience and fosters deeper intimacy with Him.

Chapter 2: Approaching God (How to Pray)

The Bible presents prayer as a dynamic encounter with God, shaped by reverence, sincerity, and a desire to commune with the Almighty. While *what prayer is* was explored in the previous chapter, the question of *how* to practice prayer warrants careful attention. In Scripture, we find patterns for preparing our hearts to pray, insights into physical postures that reflect humility or devotion, guidelines for structuring our words and intentions, and direct instruction from Jesus Himself about the manner in which we should approach the Father. This chapter aims to equip believers with practical ways to engage in meaningful prayer, recognizing that these methods serve as guides rather than rigid doctrines. Genuine prayer ultimately arises from a sincere heart aligned with God's purposes.

2.1 Preparation of the Heart

Before discussing outward expressions or specific techniques of prayer, the Bible consistently emphasizes the importance of the *inner state* of the person praying. This inward preparation sets the tone for truly communing with the Lord.

2.1.1 Confession and Forgiveness

1. **Clearing Obstacles Through Confession** Confession is more than merely listing one's sins or failings. Biblically, it involves agreeing with God about the nature of one's actions, motives, or thoughts (1 John 1:9). To "confess" (Greek: ὁμολογέω, *homologeō*) literally means to speak the same thing or be in agreement. When believers confess, they submit to God's assessment of their behavior, acknowledging that sin is a barrier to fellowship. Psalm 66:18 poignantly declares, "If I had cherished iniquity in my heart, the Lord would not have listened." Unconfessed sin, therefore, hinders prayer, not because God becomes unable to hear but because sin disrupts the intimacy believers need to approach Him confidently. Confession is not about living in perpetual guilt; rather, it is an invitation to pursue restoration. The Bible promises that God is gracious and just, willing to cleanse and forgive when sin is sincerely confessed. This spiritual cleansing opens the way for honest communication. The believer no longer hides behind shame or excuses but stands transparently before a God who knows every secret. Such transparency fosters a deeper sense of liberation and peace.

2. **Practicing Forgiveness and Reconciliation** Just as confession addresses the vertical dimension (our relationship with God), forgiveness addresses the horizontal dimension (our relationships with other people). Jesus teaches that believers must reconcile with others before presenting offerings to God (Matthew 5:23–24). If resentment, bitterness, or unresolved conflict marks a believer's relationships, these attitudes can poison the spirit, impeding sincere prayer. Mark 11:25 reads, "And whenever you stand praying, forgive, if you have anything

against anyone, so that your Father also who is in heaven may forgive you your trespasses." The principle here is straightforward: a heart harboring unforgiveness lacks the openness required for genuine communion with God. Forgiveness does not trivialize wrongdoing or minimize pain. Rather, it releases the offended person from the destructive power of grudges, mirroring the grace God extends. When believers extend forgiveness, they align with God's own character, dissolving barriers that hamper authentic prayer. Hence, a crucial aspect of *how* to pray involves ensuring one's heart is free from bitterness and that relationships remain unencumbered by unresolved conflict.

3. **Practical Steps Toward Confession and Forgiveness**

   o **Self-Examination**: Before praying, take a moment to invite the Holy Spirit to reveal any hidden sins or lingering bitterness (Psalm 139:23–24).

   o **Express Regret and Repentance**: A True confession includes a repentant attitude—desiring to turn away from sin rather than merely acknowledging it.

   o **Seek Restoration**: If possible, seek to make amends with anyone wronged, whether through an apology, restitution, or open dialogue.

   o **Rest on God's Promises**: Remember that God's grace abounds, and He is more than willing to restore fellowship once sin is confessed (Isaiah 1:18).

By making confession and forgiveness central in prayer, believers ensure that their hearts remain a fertile ground for a genuine encounter with God.

2.1.2 Humility and Reverence

1. **Biblical Basis for Humility** Scripture repeatedly exalts humility as a prerequisite for drawing near to God. James 4:6 proclaims, "God opposes the proud but gives grace to the humble." When approaching the Creator of heaven and earth, an attitude of self-exaltation or entitlement is incompatible with prayer. Instead, recognizing God's sovereignty compels a heart posture of submission, awe, and reliance. One of the most striking depictions of humility in prayer appears in the parable of the Pharisee and the tax collector (Luke 18:9–14). The Pharisee boasts of his religiosity, while the tax collector, standing far off, beats his chest and cries for mercy. Jesus declares that the repentant tax collector, not the self-righteous Pharisee, goes home justified. Such a contrast underscores that no amount of religious knowledge, discipline, or outward show of piety supplants the essential requirement of a humble heart.

2. **Expressions of Reverence** Reverence in prayer indicates a profound respect and honor for God's holiness. It naturally arises when believers grasp the magnitude of God's character: His majesty, righteousness, and mercy. Though prayer is an intimate act, it must never deteriorate into casual disregard for the One who is supremely holy (Isaiah 6:3). While reverence includes an internal posture of awe, it can also be expressed externally. Some believers choose to bow, kneel, or even prostrate themselves when praying in private, physically indicating their deep respect. Although these physical expressions are discussed more fully in Section 2.2, they stem from an inward attitude of reverence. Likewise, using biblical titles or names of God (e.g., Yahweh, Adonai, Father) with a sense of gravity can cultivate reverence. One does not invoke God's name

flippantly, for His name is holy (Exodus 20:7).

3. **Guarding Against Presumption** Humility and reverence also mean praying without presumption. This does not deny that believers can approach God boldly (Hebrews 4:16); rather, it warns against treating the privilege of access as an entitlement. The childlike confidence Jesus encourages (Matthew 7:7–11) coexists with the recognition that God is infinitely greater than His creation. Praying with reverence acknowledges that every good gift, including the privilege of being heard by God, arises from His grace rather than our merit.

4. **Practical Ways to Cultivate Humility and Reverence**

   o **Reflect on God's Character**: Meditate on passages highlighting God's holiness, sovereignty, and love (e.g., Isaiah 40; Psalm 103).

   o **Acknowledge Dependence**: Begin prayer with an admission that one's very breath and ability to speak come from God.

   o **Limit Self-Focus**: While God invites personal requests, incorporating worship and thanksgiving helps keep the prayer from becoming self-centered.

   o **Learn from Biblical Prayers**: Study prayers of humble figures like Daniel (Daniel 9:3–19) to see how they exalt God's character while confessing human frailty.

By intentionally cultivating humility and reverence, believers prepare their hearts to encounter God in a manner that honors His holiness and invites His transforming grace.

2.2 Methods and Postures

The Bible provides diverse examples of how people physically posture themselves in prayer, as well as whether they pray silently or aloud. While the internal attitude of the heart remains paramount, the outward expression can reinforce and reflect the humility, earnestness, or fervency of one's approach to God.

2.2.1 Standing, Kneeling, and Prostration

1. **Standing in Prayer** Standing is a common posture for prayer in both Jewish and early Christian traditions. In many passages, we see references to people standing before the Lord. Jesus Himself said in Mark 11:25, "And whenever you stand praying, forgive." Standing can convey respect, as one would stand before a dignitary or king. It may also reflect readiness and vigilance, symbolizing a believer's alertness in God's presence. Some Christian communities continue to stand during liturgical prayers or worship services. This posture can help individuals stay mentally engaged, reaffirming the seriousness of addressing the Almighty. Yet standing does not necessarily equate to pride; it can be a posture of reverential attention, akin to how an attentive servant stands ready to receive instructions.

2. **Kneeling in Prayer** Kneeling is perhaps the most frequently portrayed prayer posture in Christian practice. Biblically, kneeling reflects humility and submission. King Solomon knelt before the entire assembly of Israel to dedicate the Temple (2 Chronicles 6:13). Daniel knelt three times a day to pray, even under threat of persecution (Daniel 6:10). In the New Testament, the apostle Paul mentions kneeling in prayer, particularly when praying with or for fellow believers (Acts 20:36). By lowering one's body, kneeling visually communicates a heart bowed low in reverence. It

acknowledges the authority of God and the believer's dependence on Him. Many find that the act of kneeling also helps them concentrate, as it physically removes distractions and focuses the mind on God's throne of grace. However, like all postures, kneeling without genuine humility can become an empty gesture. The posture is most meaningful when it mirrors the sincerity of one's spirit.

3. **Prostration** Prostration (lying face down on the ground) is the most extreme bodily posture of humility. It appears in Scripture during moments of deep repentance, intense worship, or profound distress. For instance, Joshua fell on his face before the ark of the LORD after Israel's defeat at Ai (Joshua 7:6). In the New Testament, the apostle John fell at the feet of the risen Christ as though dead (Revelation 1:17). This posture signifies total surrender, an acknowledgment that in the presence of the holy God, human beings stand in absolute need. While prostration is not commonly practiced in every Christian tradition, it remains a valid biblical expression. In moments of acute repentance or overwhelming awe, some believers find lying prostrate to be the most fitting way to express their submission to God's majesty. As with all outward expressions, though, it should arise naturally from the heart rather than be done for show.

4. **Practical Considerations**

   o **Cultural Context:** Different Christian denominations and cultural contexts have unique customs regarding posture in prayer. None should be treated as superior or inferior if done with a right heart.

   o **Physical Limitations:** Some individuals may have

health restrictions that make kneeling or prostration difficult. Scripture never teaches that God favors one posture over another; it is the sincerity within that matters.

- o **Home or Corporate Settings**: Kneeling or prostrating is often easier to practice in private. In corporate settings, communal norms and space constraints may shape what postures are feasible.

Ultimately, the posture believers choose can enhance their prayer experience by reinforcing the attitudes of reverence and submission. However, it is always the heart posture that truly determines whether prayer honors God.

2.2.2 Silent Prayer vs. Spoken Prayer

1. **Biblical Examples of Silent Prayer** Silent prayer has a venerable history in the Bible. One of the most vivid instances is Hannah's prayer for a child (1 Samuel 1:13). She spoke in her heart; her lips moved, but her voice was not heard. Though onlookers misunderstood her, God did not. Scripture testifies that He heard the cry of her heart and answered her request with the birth of Samuel. Silent prayer can be particularly fitting in moments of deep sorrow, reflection, or when words fail us. It acknowledges that God can perceive the unspoken groans of the heart (Romans 8:26–27). Silence may also help believers cultivate interior stillness, clearing distractions to focus entirely on God's presence. In communal worship, silent prayer periods allow the congregation to reflect and personally respond to the Spirit's leading.

2. **Biblical Examples of Spoken Prayer** Spoken prayers appear throughout Scripture, from Moses's dialogues with God to

Jesus's high-priestly prayer in John 17. The Book of Psalms, too, can be understood as an anthology of prayers often intended to be sung or recited aloud. Speaking prayer aloud can serve several purposes:

- o **Vocalizing Faith**: Articulating words can cement one's trust in God. By affirming aloud the promises of Scripture or praising God's attributes, faith may be strengthened.

- o **Communal Harmony**: Spoken or sung prayers unite believers who collectively voice their worship, thanksgiving, or requests. This is common in congregational settings.

- o **Clarity of Thought**: Sometimes, formulating words aloud helps organize one's thoughts and emotions before God.

3. Jesus Himself prayed audibly on several notable occasions. In John 11:41–42, He prays openly at Lazarus's tomb, explicitly stating that He speaks aloud for the benefit of the bystanders. This moment illustrates how spoken prayer can edify others who witness a believer's faith in action.

4. **Balancing Silent and Spoken Prayer** Both silent and spoken prayer have their place in a balanced spiritual life. Some situations may call for reverent, private communion with God, while others invite vocal participation or verbal intercession. There is no biblical mandate that believers must always speak or always remain silent. Rather, the key is discerning which mode best expresses genuine devotion and aligns with the moment's context. In personal devotion, many believers combine silence and speaking, moving fluidly between silent listening and heartfelt verbal

expression.

5. **Practical Guidelines**

   o **Consider the Setting**: In shared or public contexts, voiced prayers can foster unity and understanding. In solitary reflection, silence might better cultivate contemplation.

   o **Respect Others**: In group prayer, ensure that spoken prayers remain mindful of communal participation (e.g., not overly long or monopolizing).

   o **Seek Authenticity**: Whether silent or spoken, prayer should reflect sincerity rather than conform to expectations or traditions for their own sake.

Ultimately, the Bible portrays both silent and spoken prayer as valid, powerful ways to approach God. One is not more "spiritual" than the other; each can enrich the believer's experience of communion with the Lord, provided it flows from a true desire to connect with Him.

2.3 Structure of a Prayer

While prayer is not strictly formulaic, many believers find that following a scriptural framework aids focus and balance. One common approach to structuring prayer is remembered by the acronym "ACTS": Adoration, Confession, Thanksgiving, and Supplication. Though variations exist, this pattern captures core elements frequently seen in biblical prayers.

2.3.1 Adoration (Praising God)

1. **Foundational Aspect of Adoration** Adoration, or praise, turns the believer's attention from self to God's majesty. In

biblical prayers, praise often precedes requests. For example, the psalmists regularly begin with exaltations of God's attributes—His holiness, strength, or lovingkindness—before delving into petitions or confessions (Psalm 96:1–6). This opening posture of adoration cultivates reverence and sets the prayer on a God-centered trajectory.

2. **Why Adoration Is Essential**

   o **Realigns Perspective**: Declaring who God is renews the mind, reminding believers that they pray to an almighty, compassionate Lord rather than an impersonal force.

   o **Stirs Faith**: By recounting God's attributes—His faithfulness, omnipotence, or grace—believers build confidence for the requests that follow.

   o **Honors God**: Ultimately, adoration glorifies God, acknowledging that He alone is worthy of worship.

3. **Practical Expressions of Adoration**

   o **Scriptural Praise**: Incorporate verses like Psalm 145 or Revelation 4:8 that extol God's holiness or power.

   o **Attributes of God**: Focus on a specific attribute (e.g., God's mercy), contemplating its significance and expressing gratitude for it.

   o **Singing**: In both personal and corporate prayer, songs of worship can serve as heartfelt expressions of adoration.

2.3.2 Confession (Acknowledging Sin)

1. **Link Between Adoration and Confession** Once believers perceive God's holiness through adoration, they become more aware of their sinfulness. Confession flows naturally from this realization. While a thorough discussion of confession was addressed in Section 2.1.1 regarding the preparation of the heart, it also occupies a structural position within the prayer sequence. Adoration exalts God's perfection; confession admits human imperfection.

2. **Examples of Confessional Prayers** Many scriptural prayers contain confessional elements. Psalm 51 is a classic example in which David acknowledges his wrongdoing before God and seeks purification. Daniel 9:4–19 similarly illustrates how confession can be both personal and communal, as he confesses the nation's sins.

3. **Confession Leading to Cleansing** Following confession in a structured prayer sequence invites renewed intimacy with God. The heart that acknowledges sin and pleads for mercy does so in the confidence of God's forgiving nature (Psalm 86:5). Structurally, confession prepares the way for authentic fellowship and sets the stage for gratitude.

2.3.3 Thanksgiving (Expressing Gratitude)

1. **Biblical Mandate to Give Thanks** Scripture exhorts believers to practice thanksgiving (1 Thessalonians 5:18). Giving thanks recognizes that every good and perfect gift ultimately comes from God (James 1:17). By regularly expressing gratitude, believers cultivate an attitude of contentment and trust. This gratitude spans temporal blessings—health, relationships, daily sustenance—as well as spiritual blessings such as redemption and the promise of eternal life.

2. **Thanksgiving as a Bridge in Prayer** Thanksgiving often bridges the confessional segment and the supplicatory segment. After laying sin before the Lord, believers can rejoice in the assurance of pardon. Furthermore, recalling God's past faithfulness stirs faith for present requests. The Israelite practice of memorial stones (Joshua 4:5–7) exemplifies how reflecting on past acts of God fosters gratitude and confidence in ongoing petitions.

3. **Practical Forms of Thanksgiving**

   o **Thanking God for Who He Is**: Express gratitude for God's character, such as His love, patience, and unwavering faithfulness.

   o **Recalling Specific Blessings**: Enumerate blessings—provision, protection, answered prayers, spiritual growth—and thank God by name for each.

   o **Collective Thanksgiving**: In group settings, communal testimonies and expressions of thanks can strengthen the community's faith.

2.3.4 Supplication (Presenting Requests)

1. **Definition and Scope of Supplication** Supplication involves placing one's needs, desires, and burdens before God. It encompasses petitions (requests for oneself) and intercessions (requests made on behalf of others). Scriptural examples abound, from Abraham's intercession for Sodom (Genesis 18:22–33) to the early church praying for Peter's release from prison (Acts 12:5).

2. **Confidence in Making Requests** The Bible encourages believers to approach God boldly with their requests

(Philippians 4:6–7). Having adored God's character, confessed sin, and expressed gratitude, the believer is now in a posture that acknowledges both God's ability to answer and the believer's dependence. This confidence, however, is tempered by submission to God's will (1 John 5:14). Mature supplication aligns desires with God's purposes, seeking not merely personal gain but the advancement of God's kingdom.

3. **Practical Tips for Effective Supplication**

   o **Specificity**: Clearly articulate needs or situations; vague prayers can result in vague expectations.

   o **Faith-Filled Language**: Pray with trust in God's power and willingness. Avoid self-defeating language that undermines confidence.

   o **Balanced Perspective**: Even in pressing circumstances, remember to reaffirm that God's wisdom is supreme. "Not my will, but yours, be done" (Luke 22:42).

By weaving together adoration, confession, thanksgiving, and supplication, believers can experience a well-rounded prayer life. This structure guards against neglecting core aspects—exalting God, acknowledging sin, expressing gratitude, and casting cares upon the Lord.

2.4 Jesus's Teaching on Prayer

The most definitive guidance on *how* to pray emerges from Jesus's own teaching. From His instructions in the Sermon on the Mount to His parables underscoring persistence, Jesus provides a clear roadmap for approaching the Father sincerely and effectively.

2.4.1 The Lord's Prayer as a Model

1. **Context of the Lord's Prayer** Found in Matthew 6:9–13 and again in a shortened form in Luke 11:2–4, the Lord's Prayer arises within Jesus's broader instruction on living righteously. Jesus warns against ostentatious prayer aimed at impressing others (Matthew 6:5) and against mindless repetition (Matthew 6:7). Instead, He provides a concise model that addresses all essential aspects of prayer. While the Lord's Prayer can be recited verbatim, its greater importance lies in illustrating the elements that can shape a believer's own prayers.

2. **Breakdown of the Lord's Prayer**

   - **Address: "Our Father in heaven" (Matthew 6:9)** Jesus invites believers to recognize God's paternal relationship—He is our Father, yet also reigns from heaven. This dual emphasis fosters intimacy and reverence.

   - **Worship: "Hallowed be your name" (Matthew 6:9)** This phrase underscores adoration, acknowledging the holiness of God and setting the prayer's initial focus on God's glory rather than human needs.

   - **Surrender to God's Reign: "Your kingdom come, your will be done" (Matthew 6:10)** Prayer is not about bending God to human desires; it is about aligning human hearts with God's will and longing for the fulfillment of His kingdom purposes.

   - **Dependence for Provision: "Give us this day our daily bread" (Matthew 6:11)** Jesus teaches believers to trust God for daily needs—physical, emotional, spiritual—rather than stockpiling anxious concerns for the future.

- o **Confession and Forgiveness: "Forgive us our debts, as we also have forgiven our debtors" (Matthew 6:12)** Echoing the principle in Section 2.1.1, Jesus links receiving forgiveness from God with granting forgiveness to others. The believer remains mindful of grace and the need for reconciliation.

- o **Guidance and Protection: "Lead us not into temptation, but deliver us from evil" (Matthew 6:13)** Recognizing human frailty, Jesus instructs His disciples to seek God's guidance and protection from sin and the evil one.

- o **Praise (Doxology):** Many manuscripts include a concluding doxology: "For yours is the kingdom and the power and the glory forever. Amen." Though its presence varies in modern translations, it reiterates that God deserves ultimate praise and sovereignty.

3. **Applying the Lord's Prayer Today**

- o **Personalizing the Outline**: Believers can use each clause as a springboard. For instance, "Our Father in heaven" can lead to praises of God's attributes and an acknowledgment of His fatherly care.

- o **Avoiding Empty Repetition**: Jesus did not intend for these words to become rote incantations; rather, they serve as a template capturing essential themes.

- o **A Communal Dimension**: Notably, Jesus uses *we*

and *us* rather than *I* or *me*, implying prayer's communal aspect. Even when praying privately, one can remember the broader body of Christ.

The Lord's Prayer, thus, stands as a concise yet profound model that embodies adoration, submission, reliance, confession, and the longing for God's reign—all principles that inform *how* believers should approach God in prayer.

2.4.2 Parables Illustrating Persistence

1. **The Parable of the Persistent Widow (Luke 18:1–8)** Jesus introduces this parable by explicitly stating its purpose: "to the effect that they ought always to pray and not lose heart" (Luke 18:1). The narrative describes a widow repeatedly asking for justice from a godless judge. Although the judge initially refuses, he eventually grants her request due to her persistence. Jesus then contrasts this unjust judge with God, who is infinitely more just and loving. If an unrighteous judge responds to persistent appeals, how much more will God respond to His children's fervent, ongoing prayers? Persistence, in this context, does not imply that believers must coerce a reluctant God. Rather, it showcases that tenacity in prayer cultivates faith and dependence. The prolonged process can refine the believer's motives, deepen reliance, and sharpen the focus on God's ultimate wisdom in granting the request at the right time.

2. **The Parable of the Friend at Midnight (Luke 11:5–13)** In this story, a man unexpectedly receives visitors late at night and goes to his friend's house to request bread. The friend initially objects—he and his family are in bed—but eventually complies because of the man's "impudence" or "shameless persistence." Jesus concludes with the

exhortation: "Ask, and it will be given to you; seek, and you will find; knock, and it will be opened to you" (Luke 11:9). As with the widow's parable, the point is not to suggest that God is reluctant or irritated by late-night petitions. Instead, Jesus's teaching highlights the importance of bold, expectant prayer, urging believers to keep asking, seeking, and knocking. Such persistence arises from knowing that the One who hears these prayers is good and generous. The rhetorical question in Luke 11:11—"What father among you, if his son asks for a fish, will instead of a fish give him a serpent?"—underscores that God's responses outstrip human parental care in kindness and appropriateness.

3. **Practical Lessons on Persistence**

   o **Steadfastness**: Persistent prayer is not about repetition for its own sake; it is a testament to unwavering faith.

   o **Refined Desires**: As believers persist, they often gain clarity on whether their request aligns with God's will. Over time, God may reshape or purify the request itself.

   o **Encouragement in Delay**: When answers do not materialize immediately, the parables remind believers that apparent delay does not equate to divine disinterest. God's timing is always purposeful.

In sum, Jesus's parables on persistence bolster the "how" of prayer by revealing that believers should not be timid or give up easily. Instead, they can approach God with resolute confidence, trusting that He hears and responds in ways that foster spiritual growth and bring glory to His name.

2.5 Extended Reflections on "How to Pray"

Having explored preparation of the heart, the significance of outward postures and methods, a scriptural structure for prayer, and Jesus's direct instructions, we can draw together several overarching reflections. These insights reinforce the idea that "how to pray" involves both external practice and internal posture, all rooted in a living relationship with God.

1. **Balance Between Structure and Spontaneity** A structured approach—such as the ACTS outline or the Lord's Prayer—offers a helpful framework that ensures essential elements like praise, repentance, gratitude, and petitions are all covered. On the other hand, prayer in Scripture also bursts forth spontaneously, as seen in Nehemiah's "arrow prayers" (Nehemiah 2:4–5). Thus, a healthy prayer life need not be rigidly formulaic. Believers can benefit from both carefully planned, structured times of prayer and spontaneous, heartfelt appeals throughout the day.

2. **Ongoing Growth in Prayer Technique** Although the heart's attitude is paramount, believers can continually refine their "technique" or approach to prayer. Learning from biblical prayers, reading about historical prayer practices within the Church, and interacting with other believers can enrich one's own methods. Far from being an academic exercise, growing in *how* one prays is part of discipleship. The disciples themselves asked Jesus, "Lord, teach us to pray" (Luke 11:1). This humble request implies that learning the art of prayer is a gradual, ongoing process.

3. **Sensitivity to the Holy Spirit** In Romans 8:26–27, Paul speaks about the Holy Spirit aiding believers in prayer, especially when words or direction fail. A structured approach does not replace the Spirit's guidance; rather, it can work in harmony with it. The Holy Spirit may prompt a

sudden need for confession, direct attention to a neglected area of thanksgiving, or impress upon a believer the urgency of intercession for a specific person or situation. Being attentive to such promptings refines *how* we pray, ensuring that prayer remains relational and Spirit-led rather than mechanical.

4. **Context Shapes Method** The Bible does not enforce a single "correct" method of prayer for all believers and all circumstances. Instead, it provides multiple examples— some worshipful and contemplative, others fervent and urgent, still others silent and meditative. Hence, the manner of prayer will often change depending on one's context: private devotion versus public worship, crisis moments versus routine daily prayer, or joyful celebration versus mourning. Flexibility and discernment become crucial.

5. **Corporate vs. Private Prayer** *How* one prays in a group setting may differ from private devotions. In corporate worship, prayers may be voiced aloud for collective edification (1 Corinthians 14:16–17). In personal prayer, however, believers may opt for greater vulnerability and extended silence. While both forms are vital, each context calls for unique considerations. Group prayers often benefit from succinctness and clarity to accommodate communal participation, whereas personal prayers can be more expansive and meandering.

6. **Guarding Against Ritualism** When discussing "how" to pray, there is a subtle risk of sliding into legalism or ritualism—ticking off boxes as though fulfilling a checklist. The underlying principle, however, is that these methods serve as guides, not chains. If a believer clings to a given posture or formula without the corresponding heart

engagement, prayer degenerates into empty routine. Jesus's denunciation of "vain repetitions" (Matthew 6:7) underscores that God looks beyond external form. The *heart* behind each method matters most.

7. **Practical Aids to Enhance Focus** Many believers find practical aids beneficial for staying focused on God while praying. Some keep a prayer journal, noting praises, confessions, requests, and answered prayers. Others use biblical devotionals that provide daily structures or themes for prayer. Some practice "praying Scripture" by paraphrasing psalms or epistles as personal prayers. These tools can enrich the practical *how* of prayer while helping believers remain attentive and intentional.

8. **Continual Alignment with God's Will** "How to pray" is never disjoin from the question of alignment with God's will. In 1 John 5:14, believers are reminded that if they ask anything according to God's will, He hears them. Thus, the process of structuring prayer—adoration, confession, thanksgiving, supplication—helps realign the believer's heart with God's priorities. Adoration magnifies His attributes, confession removes barriers, thanksgiving shifts focus to His faithfulness, and supplication seeks divine help in a context shaped by surrender. This cyclical movement fosters spiritual maturity, as the believer increasingly prays God-centered prayers rather than merely self-centered ones.

9. **Developing Perseverance in Prayer** How believers pray also involves *persistence*, as highlighted in Jesus's parables. Spiritual perseverance is nurtured over time. Believers learn to keep returning to the throne of grace, refusing discouragement when immediate results are not visible. This perseverance refines motives, grows faith, and yields

deeper intimacy with God. By embracing the biblical call to "pray without ceasing" (1 Thessalonians 5:17), Christians cultivate a lifestyle of prayer rather than confining prayer to sporadic or crisis-only events.

10. **Holistic Integration** Ultimately, the biblical teachings on *how* to pray reveal that prayer is comprehensive, affecting body, soul, and spirit. Bodily postures (standing, kneeling, prostrating) reinforce internal postures (humility, reverence). Structured patterns (ACTS, the Lord's Prayer) blend with free-flowing expressions. Silent reflection complements voiced petitions. Preparation of the heart through confession and a willingness to forgive sets the tone for meaningful communion with God. Jesus's model prayer and parables on persistence further underscore the continuity between the believer's inner transformation and their outward practice of prayer.

In conclusion, approaching God in prayer involves more than selecting a posture or reciting words. It is a holistic endeavor that merges an attentive heart, physical expressions of devotion, and thoughtful structure, all underpinned by biblical instruction and Jesus's own example. Whether believers pray quietly in solitude or raise their voices in community, the essential principle is sincerity before God—coming with hearts prepared, mindful of sin and forgiveness, and confident in God's grace. By integrating these insights on how to pray, Christians can draw nearer to the Lord, experience richer fellowship, and witness the transformative power of prayer that resonates throughout Scripture and across all ages.

Chapter 3: Embracing the Prayer Life (When to Pray)

Prayer, as presented throughout Scripture, is not confined to a single time or setting. Rather, it weaves its way through every facet of a believer's daily existence and through the entire spectrum of human experience, from moments of joy to seasons of distress. This chapter addresses the rhythms, seasons, and continuous nature of prayer, urging us to see "when to pray" as both a practical consideration (e.g., morning, evening) and a theological conviction (pray *always*). By examining the Bible's teachings and examples, we discover that while certain moments are especially conducive to prayer, no moment lies outside the invitation to commune with God.

3.1 Daily Rhythms of Prayer

Throughout the Bible, we see various hints and explicit examples of believers carving out regular times to pray. These dedicated moments of each day underscore that prayer was meant to be habitual, not haphazard. Morning and evening emerge as two prominent markers of the day often associated with focused communion with the Lord. While Scripture does not prescribe rigid time slots for all believers, the principle remains: building regular prayer rhythms can nurture spiritual steadiness and deepen one's relationship with God.

3.1.1 Morning Devotions

1. **Biblical Precedent for Early Prayer** The practice of seeking God in the morning appears frequently in Scripture. In Psalm 5:3, David declares, "O LORD, in the morning you hear my voice; in the morning I prepare a sacrifice for you and watch." Here, David reveals an intentional habit of directing his prayers to God at daybreak. Psalm 63:1 similarly begins, "O God, you are my God; earnestly I seek you; my soul thirsts for you," which many interpret as a morning cry of devotion, though it can apply to any earnest pursuit of God. By lifting one's voice to God as the day dawns, the believer sets the tone for every subsequent hour. This practice underscores dependence on the Lord and recognizes that each new day is a gift from His hand. While modern life may not mirror the agrarian context of ancient Israel, the impulse to begin the day in prayer resonates across cultures and eras.

2. **Spiritual and Practical Benefits**

   o **Aligning the Heart**: Beginning in prayer helps believers surrender daily plans, aspirations, and concerns to God. This posture can minimize anxiety, reminding one that God is sovereign over the hours ahead.

   o **Nourishing the Soul**: Much like breakfast fuels the body, morning devotion "fuels" the soul. By meditating on Scripture, offering praise, or quietly listening for the Spirit's prompting, a believer finds spiritual nourishment that can sustain them through challenges.

o **Cultivating Gratitude**: The dawning of each day reflects God's faithfulness (Lamentations 3:22–23). A morning prayer of thanksgiving can frame the day in awareness of God's mercies, which are "new every morning."

3. **Examples of Morning Prayer in Action**

o **Jesus's Example**: Although the Gospels do not lock Jesus's prayer times to a strict schedule, Mark 1:35 notes that "rising very early in the morning, while it was still dark, he departed and went out to a desolate place, and there he prayed." Jesus's example underscores that the early morning can be a time of focused communion, away from the bustle of daily demands.

o **Job's Faithfulness**: In Job 1:5, we read how Job rose early to consecrate his children, offering burnt offerings on their behalf. This narrative, while focused on sacrifice and concern for family, also highlights a pattern of early-morning devotion— demonstrating awareness that intercession and worship are fitting acts at the start of the day.

4. **Practical Suggestions for Morning Prayer**

o **Find Solitude**: Waking up even a few minutes earlier can provide a precious window of solitude. Minimizing distractions—phones, emails, notifications—helps center one's heart on God.

o **Incorporate Scripture:** Reading a psalm or a short passage before praying can anchor the mind in biblical truth, shaping the content of the prayer.

o **Short But Consistent:** While extended times of morning prayer are beneficial, even short, focused prayers can yield powerful results if practiced consistently. Over time, the discipline becomes an eagerly anticipated encounter with the Lord.

In sum, morning devotions exemplify a proactive posture of inviting God into one's day. Though believers are free to choose the rhythm that suits their lifestyle, scriptural testimonies highlight the blessings of seeking God early, acknowledging Him as the foundation of all daily endeavors.

3.1.2 Evening Reflection

1. **Biblical Encouragement for Nighttime Prayer** Just as dawn marks a fresh start, dusk symbolizes the close of a day's labor and concerns. Throughout the Old Testament, believers turned to the Lord in the evening to offer praises and lay down burdens accumulated during daylight hours. In Psalm 4:8, David declares, "In peace I will both lie down and sleep; for you alone, O LORD, make me dwell in safety." This verse implies an evening trust placed in God's protective care. The practice of evening prayer also resonates with Psalm 141:2—"Let my prayer be counted as incense before you, and the lifting up of my hands as the evening sacrifice!" Incense and evening sacrifices accompanied the twilight rituals in the Temple. For modern believers, the principle remains: acknowledging God's goodness, confessing any failings, and resting in His sovereignty as the day concludes.

2. **Evening Prayer as a Spiritual Checkpoint** Evening prayer serves as a reflective gateway, allowing individuals to recount blessings, confront disappointments, and surrender tomorrow's uncertainties. By reviewing the day, believers can identify moments of divine faithfulness, areas where temptation overcame them, or instances of spiritual growth. This helps keep the conscience sensitive and fosters ongoing spiritual formation.

   o **Unburdening the Heart**: Jesus encourages casting anxieties upon God (1 Peter 5:7), and evening prayer offers an opportunity to do just that—entrusting every unresolved worry to the Father before sleep.

   o **Examining the Conscience**: A brief period of silent reflection can reveal sins or missed opportunities, prompting confessions and requests for forgiveness. This practice keeps short accounts with God, preventing guilt or bitterness from festering overnight (Ephesians 4:26).

   o **Expressing Gratitude**: Reflecting on the day's events can highlight blessings—provision, good news, unexpected kindness—thus fostering a spirit of thanksgiving as the believer drifts into rest.

3. **Biblical Examples of Evening Interaction with God**

   o **Jesus in the Evenings**: On several occasions, Jesus stayed up late in prayer, or He sent His disciples ahead while He went to a mountain to pray (Matthew 14:23). Though not explicitly labeled as "evening prayer times," these stories illustrate that Jesus utilized quiet, end-of-day hours for extended communion with the Father.

- o **Daniel's Pattern:** While Daniel is often noted for praying three times a day (Daniel 6:10), his practice almost certainly included evening prayer. Though Scripture does not parse out each specific time, Daniel's disciplined routine suggests that twilight offered a natural time for reflection and invocation.

4. **Incorporating Evening Prayer in Modern Life**

- o **Bedtime Ritual:** Instead of concluding the day with screens or social media, setting aside a few moments for focused prayer can recalibrate the heart.

- o **Family Devotions:** In many households, gathering as a family at night to read Scripture or voice collective thanksgivings can reinforce unity and mutual support.

- o **Journaling:** Writing down the day's reflections, praises, and concerns can help track spiritual progress and answered prayers.

By ending the day in fellowship with God, believers discover renewed peace and rest, confident that the One who never slumbers watches over them (Psalm 121:3–4).

3.1.3 Midday Prayer and Additional Rhythms

While morning and evening remain prominent in Scripture, other times are also highlighted as moments to pause and reconnect with God:

- • **Midday or Mealtimes:** In Acts 10:9, Peter goes to the rooftop to pray at midday, while he awaits a meal. Daniel, as previously mentioned, prayed multiple times daily (Daniel 6:10). Incorporating short prayers at noon or during lunch breaks can provide spiritual recalibration amidst busyness.

- **"Evening, Morning, and at Noon"**: Psalm 55:17 mentions these three moments specifically—"Evening and morning and at noon I utter my complaint and moan, and he hears my voice." While not prescribing a strict schedule, it reveals a pattern of multiple daily touchpoints that keep one's heart aligned with God.

- **Regular Prayer Offices**: Later church traditions (such as certain monastic orders or liturgical denominations) developed "offices" or fixed-hour prayers, influencing Christian practice for centuries. While these are not biblically mandated, they reflect an outworking of the scriptural principle of *continual* prayer.

For the modern believer, embracing daily rhythms of prayer need not be legalistic. Rather, it is an invitation to build a life where communion with God is as regular as the rising sun or the closing of the day. Whether one's schedule is traditional (morning, evening) or more flexible, intentionally setting aside time for prayer reorients the soul toward God.

3.2 Praying in All Seasons

Life's circumstances fluctuate. The Bible's pages teem with stories of individuals turning to God in desperate trials and jubilant victories alike.

3.2.1 Times of Crisis and Need

1. **Biblical Examples of Praying in Crisis**

o **Jonah in the Fish (Jonah 2:1–10)**: Swallowed by a great fish and believing himself near death, Jonah cried out from within the depths of the sea. God heard his cry, demonstrating that even when believers feel trapped—whether literally or metaphorically—divine assistance remains available.

o **Hezekiah's Plea (2 Kings 19:14–20)**: When King Sennacherib of Assyria threatened Jerusalem, Hezekiah spread the threatening letter before the Lord in the Temple. His urgent plea for deliverance exemplifies how crisis can propel one into fervent, focused prayer.

o **The Early Church (Acts 12:5)**: With Peter imprisoned and facing likely execution, the church prayed "earnestly" for him. Their unified petitions preceded an angelic intervention, underscoring how collective cries to God can yield dramatic divine responses.

2. **Why Prayer Is Crucial in Crisis**

o **Immediate Dependence**: Crisis strips away illusions of self-sufficiency. Whether facing illness, financial strain, or familial strife, prayer in such times acknowledges that God alone can bring true resolution or comfort.

o **Perspective Shift**: Petitioning God in distress can recalibrate the believer's view, turning panic into trust. Scriptural laments (e.g., many Psalms) illustrate that honest expressions of anguish still coexist with hope, as the psalmist directs suffering toward the One able to redeem it.

- o **Invitation to Faith**: In crisis, the believer stands at a crossroads—either yielding to despair or leaning into faith. Prayer becomes an act of faith: a demonstration that one trusts God's character, even when circumstances appear grim (Psalm 56:3–4).

3. **Practical Considerations for Crisis Prayer**

- o **Authentic Cry**: Scripture does not downplay emotional turmoil; prayers of desperation can be raw and unfiltered, echoing biblical lament. Honest transparency invites God's comfort.

- o **Community Support**: While private prayer remains vital, seeking prayer support from friends or church members can provide strength (Galatians 6:2).

- o **Regular Persistence**: Crisis can persist beyond a single prayer session. Maintaining persistent prayer, as Jesus illustrated in the parable of the persistent widow (Luke 18:1–8), can fortify hope over the long haul.

- o **Worship Amid Trial**: Even in crisis, praising God for who He is (apart from current troubles) can foster resilience. This does not trivialize suffering; it anchors faith in the unchanging character of God.

3.2.2 Times of Celebration and Joy

1. **Biblical Examples of Prayer in Celebration**

- o **Hannah's Thanksgiving (1 Samuel 2:1–10)**: After God granted her request for a child, Hannah lifted a jubilant prayer of praise, extolling the Lord's sovereignty and goodness. This illustrates how answered prayers should be met with thankfulness.

- o **Mary's Magnificat (Luke 1:46–55)**: Learning she would bear the Messiah, Mary responded with an outpouring of worship. Her prayer-poem, known as the Magnificat, exalts God's mercy and faithfulness to His people.

- o **The Dedicatory Prayer (2 Chronicles 7:1–3)**: When Solomon finished praying at the Temple's dedication, "fire came down from heaven" and "the glory of the LORD filled the temple." The people bowed in worship, celebrating God's presence and blessings.

2. **Purpose of Celebration Prayers**

- o **Acknowledging Divine Provision**: Joyful prayer gives credit where it is due—recognizing God as the ultimate source of blessings (James 1:17). Celebrations of new life, answered supplication, or personal milestones become testimonies to the Lord's kindness.

- o **Sustaining Spiritual Vitality**: Gratitude and celebration deepen spiritual maturity. When believers habitually thank God, they remain mindful of His ongoing work, fostering a posture of expectancy for future grace.

- o **Sharing Corporate Joy**: In biblical narrative, gatherings often included public prayers of thanksgiving. Such communal expressions unite believers in mutual encouragement. Testimonies of God's goodness can stir praise among all who hear (Psalm 34:3).

3. **Practical Suggestions for Celebration Prayer**

   o **Marking Milestones**: Whether a wedding, the birth of a child, a birthday, or a new job, intentionally pausing to pray fosters recognition that God orchestrates good gifts.

   o **Creative Expressions**: Celebratory prayers can be sung (as many biblical hymns and psalms were), written as poems, or shared in community. This creativity can intensify worship and preserve memories for future reflection.

   o **Balanced Gratitude**: Even in joy, believers can remain mindful of others' needs, interceding for those who are grieving. Celebration prayer does not ignore suffering but radiates hope that can comfort others.

Scripture depicts believers crying out to God in dire straits and erupting in praise when deliverance or blessing arrives. Recognizing this full emotional range underscores the adaptability and comprehensiveness of prayer—God welcomes His people's petitions and praises in every season.

3.3 Continuous Prayer

Beyond designated times (morning, evening, or crisis) lies a deeper biblical principle: the call to perpetual communion with God. The Apostle Paul's exhortation to "pray without ceasing" (1 Thessalonians 5:17) is perhaps the clearest articulation of this notion. At first glance, praying "constantly" can sound hyperbolic— surely daily tasks, conversations, and responsibilities demand attention. Yet Scripture suggests that continuous prayer is less about unending monologue and more about maintaining a prayerful *disposition*—an ongoing awareness of and reliance upon the presence of God.

3.3.1 Living in an Attitude of Prayer

1. **Biblical Foundation**

   o **1 Thessalonians 5:16–18**: "Rejoice always, pray without ceasing, give thanks in all circumstances." This trio of commands indicates that prayerfulness, joy, and gratitude should permeate every dimension of a believer's life.

   o **Ephesians 6:18**: Paul urges believers to be "praying at all times in the Spirit," underlining prayer as integral to the spiritual warfare context. It suggests that vigilance in prayer forms part of the believer's defensive and offensive arsenal against temptation and discouragement.

2. **What Continuous Prayer Looks Like** Continuous prayer does not mean one recites formal prayers every moment of the day. Instead, it entails cultivating a mental and spiritual posture wherein the heart remains open to God at all times. Believers can direct spontaneous thanksgivings or requests to God while commuting, working, studying, or relaxing. The line between "praying" and "not praying" becomes fluid, as everyday life merges seamlessly with ongoing communion.

   o **Quick, Silent Petitions**: Nehemiah's swift prayer before responding to King Artaxerxes (Nehemiah 2:4–5) exemplifies a moment of unplanned invocation, offered in the midst of a mundane activity.

- o **Conversational Approach**: Mentally sharing small thoughts, joys, or concerns with God throughout the day fosters intimacy—like walking alongside a close friend who remains engaged in all that transpires.

3. **Benefits of an Attitude of Prayer**

- o **Reduced Anxiety**: A mind that reflexively turns worries into prayers experiences less rumination on fears. Philippians 4:6–7 connects prayer with the "peace of God, which surpasses all understanding."

- o **Heightened Spiritual Sensitivity**: Constant dialogue with the Lord attunes one to gentle nudges of the Holy Spirit—perhaps leading to spontaneous acts of compassion or timely words of encouragement.

- o **Greater Reliance on God**: The more consistently one prays, the more one senses God's nearness, diminishing the drive for self-sufficiency. Over time, this nurtures an authentic dependence on God's guidance.

4. **Practical Strategies for Fostering Unceasing Prayer**

- o **Prayer Triggers**: Some believers associate certain tasks—washing dishes, walking to the car, hearing a text message alert—with short prayers of thanks or requests for guidance.

- o **Scripture Reminders**: Placing sticky notes with

verses in visible locations can prompt instant communion, prompting the mind and heart to respond in prayer.

- o **Digital Aids:** Setting reminders on a smartphone to pause and pray, or using apps that provide hourly Scripture prompts, can help embed prayer into one's routine.

3.3.2 Practicing the Presence of God

1. **Historical Perspective** While not directly a biblical phrase, "practicing the presence of God" describes the overarching biblical principle of consciously abiding in God's nearness (John 15:4–5). The roots of this concept appear throughout Scripture in commands such as "Set the LORD always before me" (Psalm 16:8) or "Draw near to God, and he will draw near to you" (James 4:8). In essence, the believer acknowledges God's omnipresence and chooses to live in mindful fellowship with Him.

2. **Scriptural Illustrations**

- o **Enoch and Noah:** Both are described as walking with God (Genesis 5:24; Genesis 6:9). Though details are scarce, this phrase implies an ongoing, relational closeness, likely undergirded by continual trust and communication with the Lord.

- o **Moses and the Tent of Meeting (Exodus 33:7–11):** Moses regularly entered the Tent of Meeting to converse with God "face to face, as a man speaks to his friend." While a literal location facilitated Moses's encounters, the principle of regular, intimate interaction can be applied in spiritual practice today.

3. **Practical Dimensions**

- o **Awareness of God's Involvement**: Rather than seeing daily tasks as separate from spiritual life, believers practicing God's presence recognize that each activity can be offered as service to Him (Colossians 3:17).

- o **Inner Dialogue**: This might manifest as quiet mental remarks such as "Thank you, Lord," or "Lord, guide me," or "Help me to reflect your love," woven into any moment.

- o **Reverence Coupled with Intimacy**: One essential tension in practicing God's presence is maintaining both awe (He is the holy King) and familiarity (He is the loving Father). This ensures that closeness does not breed casual irreverence but fosters heartfelt communion.

4. **Obstacles and Encouragements**

- o **Distractions**: Modern life overflows with digital notifications, tasks, and entertainment that can dilute one's awareness of God. Periodic, deliberate times of silence or "digital fasting" can nurture sensitivity to God's voice.

- o **Guilt or Anxiety**: Some believers feel unworthy to remain conscious of God's presence, particularly when they stumble. However, Scripture calls us to approach the throne of grace confidently (Hebrews 4:16), emphasizing grace rather than condemnation.

- o **Daily Renewal**: Practicing the presence of God is

not a feat accomplished overnight. It is a gradual cultivation of habit, often requiring reminders and reflection. Yet the reward is a deepening sense of peace and guidance, as the believer learns to interpret every circumstance through the lens of divine companionship.

Ultimately, the concept of continuous prayer—whether framed as an "attitude of prayer" or "practicing the presence of God"— elevates prayer from an isolated religious activity to a way of life. While designated prayer times remain valuable, Scripture affirms that every moment can be an occasion for communion with God.

3.4 Extended Reflections on "When to Pray"

Having outlined daily rhythms, the dual realities of crisis and celebration, and the call to perpetual communion, we can draw several overarching insights. These reflections will help synthesize biblical teachings on the timing of prayer:

1. **Prayer as a Lifelong Rhythm** "When to pray" extends beyond a single moment or crisis into a tapestry of daily patterns. By embracing morning gratitude, midday alignment, and evening reflection, believers anchor themselves in a spiritual routine that fosters stability and growth. While these patterns are not mandatory, their scriptural basis validates their effectiveness for many believers. Each day becomes bookended by acknowledgment of God's mercy at dawn and reflection on His faithfulness at dusk.

2. **Prayer as a Response to All Circumstances** Whether overwhelmed by sorrow or overflowing with praise, the believer's reflex ought to be turning to God. This underscores the inclusiveness of prayer: no mood or event disqualifies someone from seeking the Lord. The Psalms

illustrate that God welcomes laments, confessions, praises, and thanks. Thus, the question "When to pray?" finds a manifold answer: *whenever we face trials, whenever we rejoice, and in all in-between moments.*

3. **Fostering Spiritual Vigilance** A consistent "when" to pray also bolsters vigilance against temptation (Ephesians 6:18). Regular contact with God readies the heart to resist spiritual attacks. During the day's unremarkable stretches, it is easy to drift into complacency. A cultivated habit of prayer—whether through set intervals or ongoing inner dialogue—keeps the believer spiritually alert. Jesus commanded His disciples in Gethsemane to "watch and pray" (Matthew 26:41), suggesting that prayer and alertness go hand in hand.

4. **Freedom from Legalism** While Scripture showcases morning, evening, and unceasing prayer, it does not enforce a rigid timetable. Jesus rebuked the Pharisees for turning spiritual disciplines into burdensome laws (Matthew 23:1–4). Believers are free to adopt or adapt the rhythms that best align with their circumstances and God's leading. Some may discover that late-night prayer suits them, while others treasure daybreak devotions. The core principle is authenticity, not adherence to external ritual.

5. **Unity and Community** Individual prayer practices inevitably influence community life. When individuals develop consistent prayer rhythms, church gatherings often become more vibrant, as people arrive spiritually prepared to worship together. Likewise, corporate events—such as midweek prayer meetings—can become a shared "when" for communal intercession. The New Testament church models how collective prayer can galvanize unity and empower the mission of God's people

(Acts 2:42; 4:31).

6. **Continual Integration of Prayer and Life** Scripture's emphasis on praying "always" or "without ceasing" suggests that *when* to pray transcends designated intervals. Rather than relegating prayer to devotional corners, believers are to integrate it into the fabric of daily activity. Conversing with God amidst chores, traffic, or office tasks redefines these mundane moments as spiritual territory. This does not diminish the value of formal prayer times but enriches them, ensuring that prayer remains an ongoing dialogue rather than a compartmentalized practice.

7. **Hope in Waiting** At times, believers may pray earnestly without seeing immediate results. "When to pray" then also includes *the long wait*. Jesus's parable of the persistent widow (Luke 18:1–8) specifically urges believers not to lose heart. In seasons of apparent delay, continuing to pray fosters perseverance. God's timing may differ from human expectations, but unwavering prayer affirms trust in His sovereignty, even in prolonged uncertainty.

8. **Discerning God's Timing** Another facet of "when to pray" involves discerning God's timing in responding. Believers might question if certain prayers are best offered in a specific season or manner. While Scripture does not propose a hidden code for perfect "prayer timing," it does encourage sensitivity to the Holy Spirit's leading. For instance, Ecclesiastes 3:1–8 reminds us that there is "a time for every matter under heaven," hinting at the wisdom of aligning prayerful pursuits with God's seasons. Perhaps a desire for vocational change, a new ministry endeavor, or reconciliation with a loved one calls for persistent prayer over months or even years, awaiting divine release or

guidance.

9. **Joy in Variety** No single formula or pattern exhausts the Bible's teaching on *when* to pray. Some biblical figures prayed spontaneously in crises, others followed daily schedules, and still others simply walked in continuous fellowship with the Lord. This variety speaks to the richness of the Christian prayer life. Whether one thrives on structured routines or on impromptu bursts of communication with God, Scripture's overarching message is that prayer finds its place in *every* moment that touches a believer's heart.

10. **Invitation to Deeper Relationship** Ultimately, each time slot—morning, noon, evening, or ongoing—presents an invitation. "When to pray" becomes less about duty and more about friendship with God. The motivation shifts from "I *must* pray now" to "I *get* to pray now." This relational dynamic forms the heartbeat of biblical prayer: a loving God who desires fellowship, and a people who discover increasing joy and strength in turning to Him at all times.

Chapter 4: Prayers in Scripture (Number of Prayers in the Bible)

4.1 Overview of Scriptural Prayers

Any effort to count the prayers in the Bible immediately encounters the remarkable diversity of the biblical text. From historical narratives to poetry, from Gospels to epistles, prayer emerges in myriad forms and contexts. For clarity, it helps to recognize certain broad categories: **narrative prayers** found in stories, **liturgical or poetic prayers** like those in the Psalms, **prophetic prayers** embedded within prophetic books, **didactic prayers** such as those in the New Testament epistles, and **apocalyptic prayers** in books like Daniel or Revelation. While these categories inevitably overlap, they help paint a picture of how frequently—and creatively—the people of God communicated with Him.

4.1.1 Old Testament Prayers: From Genesis to Malachi

1. **Genesis and the Patriarchs** The first book of the Bible, *Genesis*, introduces prayer more by implication than by formal labels. For instance, in Genesis 4:26, Scripture notes

that people "began to call upon the name of the LORD," which many interpreters regard as an early reference to prayer. Later, Abraham pleads with God for the city of Sodom (Genesis 18:22–33), offering one of the earliest extended intercessory prayers. The text never explicitly says "Abraham prayed," yet his dialogue with God matches the essential posture of prayer: humble petition and negotiation before the Almighty. As we progress through Genesis, we see brief yet vital prayers from Isaac, Jacob, and others. Some are explicit: Jacob wrestles all night and, in effect, prays for a blessing (Genesis 32:26–29). Yet, some of these communications are not labeled "prayer" in a modern sense. They contain direct discourse with God that can be categorized as prayerful dialogue.

2. **Exodus through Deuteronomy** Moses stands as a towering figure of intercession in books like Exodus, Leviticus, Numbers, and Deuteronomy. Numerous passages depict him intervening on behalf of Israel, pleading for divine mercy when God's wrath is aroused due to the people's sin (Exodus 32:11–14; Numbers 14:13–19). Many would count each of these intercessions as a distinct prayer, yet discerning whether a certain passage constitutes one single prayer, multiple prayers, or a prayer plus a subsequent dialogue can complicate an exact tally. Additionally, Moses's own personal appeals to God—for strength, guidance, or forgiveness—sprinkle the narrative. Deuteronomy includes extensive speeches by Moses, some of which shift into prayerful exhortations. The question for counters arises: does each exhortation to the people that references God's name in an intercessory tone qualify as a prayer, or must a text explicitly show Moses addressing God directly?

3. **Historical Books (Joshua to Esther)** As we proceed through Joshua, Judges, Ruth, 1–2 Samuel, 1–2 Kings, 1–2 Chronicles, Ezra, Nehemiah, and Esther, we encounter multiple prayers embedded in historical narrative. Notable examples include Hannah's heartfelt petition for a son (1 Samuel 1:10–13), Solomon's dedication of the Temple (1 Kings 8:22–53), and the national prayers of repentance in Nehemiah (Nehemiah 9). Other prayers are personal pleas, such as Elijah's showdown on Mount Carmel (1 Kings 18:36–37) and Hezekiah's cry for deliverance from the Assyrians (2 Kings 19:14–19). While these books often recount prayers in direct speech, sometimes the text only summarizes that a given leader "inquired of the LORD," leaving it ambiguous whether we should count each inquiry as a separate prayer. Indeed, biblical references to prayer multiply when one realizes that "inquire of the LORD" typically represents seeking divine will—functionally, a prayer. If a chapter of 1 Chronicles mentions multiple inquiries, do we count each instance? Such nuances, addressed in Section 4.2, complicate attempts at enumerating prayers strictly by a uniform rule.

4. **Poetic and Wisdom Literature** The Book of Psalms is arguably the most prayer-rich portion of the Old Testament, containing psalms of lament, thanksgiving, praise, and more. While these are typically understood as songs, they also double as prayers, with many psalms explicitly directed toward God (e.g., "Hear my cry, O God..." in Psalm 61:1). If we count each psalm as a single prayer, we might quickly conclude there are 150 prayers in the Psalms alone, since each psalm in its entirety is an address to God. However, some psalms have multiple sections of petition and praise, occasionally shifting in speaker or theme. Moreover, certain psalms were penned for

communal worship, others for personal devotion, and some purely for instruction. Determining whether a portion of a psalm qualifies as a single prayer or multiple can be subjective. Besides the Psalms, Job includes extended dialogues that at times turn directly into prayers or pleas. Proverbs and Ecclesiastes rarely present explicit prayers—though a few passages, such as Proverbs 30:7–9, take the form of direct addresses to God, arguably counting as prayers.

5. **Prophetic Books (Isaiah to Malachi)** The prophets frequently intercede for Israel or engage in prayerful dialogue with God. For instance, Jeremiah's confessions (sometimes called "Jeremiah's laments," e.g., Jeremiah 20:7–18) can be read as prayerful outpourings of anguish. Daniel's well-known prayer of repentance for the nation (Daniel 9:4–19) is one of the more extended confessional prayers in the Old Testament, while Jonah 2:1–9 preserves a psalm-like prayer from the belly of the great fish. These varied presentations—dialogues, laments, oracles—reflect the intricate ways in which prayer weaves throughout the prophets. Yet again, a single prophetic passage might contain multiple prayerful utterances or revolve around a single, extended address to God.

4.1.2 New Testament Prayers: From the Gospels to Revelation

1. **Prayer in the Gospels** Though we do not revisit the *methods* of Jesus's prayers (as covered in a previous chapter on how to pray), we note that the four Gospels (Matthew, Mark, Luke, John) are replete with scenes where Jesus prays—alone, in public, before miracles, after miracles, and even on the cross. Beyond Jesus, we see characters like the father of the demon-possessed boy, who cries out in desperation, "I believe; help my unbelief!"

(Mark 9:24)—a short but heartfelt petition. Counting the prayers of Jesus alone could be an extensive endeavor: do we list each distinct prayer found in the Gospels, such as the Lord's Prayer (Matthew 6:9–13), the High Priestly Prayer (John 17), or the brief prayers of thanksgiving before feeding crowds (e.g., Matthew 14:19)? Each is a unique instance of prayer. Meanwhile, many people in the Gospels also address Jesus with requests that arguably function like prayers—though they address the Son of God, the text portrays these as requests for healing rather than prayer in the strict sense. Such borderline cases highlight why enumerating prayers can be tricky.

2. **Acts of the Apostles and the Early Church** After the Gospels, the Book of Acts documents how the early believers prayed at pivotal moments, from communal supplication in Acts 1:14 as they awaited the Holy Spirit, to the outcry in Acts 4:24–31 for boldness after persecution, to personal prayers like Paul's experience following his Damascus Road encounter (Acts 9:11). Each instance underscores the formative role of prayer in launching and guiding the early church. Acts portrays both communal prayers (e.g., when the apostles and believers gathered in a house to petition God for Peter's release in Acts 12:5) and individual prayers (e.g., Cornelius praying at the ninth hour in Acts 10:30). Some references are explicit about "praying," while others state that believers "called on the name of the Lord" (Acts 9:14). Deciding how to count each reference, or whether some references blend into extended narratives, is not straightforward.

3. **Pauline Epistles and Other Letters** Paul's letters—Romans, 1–2 Corinthians, Galatians, Ephesians, and so forth—often begin or conclude with prayerful expressions or

benedictions. Paul frequently writes phrases like "I do not cease to give thanks for you, remembering you in my prayers" (Ephesians 1:16). Are these simply references to Paul's ongoing prayer life, or do we treat them as explicit prayers when he transitions into direct petition, such as "that the God of our Lord Jesus Christ... may give you the Spirit of wisdom" (Ephesians 1:17–19)? These epistolary prayers typically combine teaching with genuine intercession. Similarly, Peter, John, James, and the author of Hebrews offer prayerful asides or doxologies throughout their writings (e.g., Hebrews 13:20–21). While we may categorize such passages as "teaching about prayer," many are themselves expressions of prayer on behalf of the audience. This dual function—both instructive and supplicatory—can obscure a neat count.

4. **Revelation and Apocalyptic Prayers** The Book of Revelation contains worshipful prayers and doxologies offered by heavenly beings, saints, and angels (Revelation 4:8–11; 5:9–14; 7:9–17). John also depicts the prayers of the martyrs (Revelation 6:9–10) who cry out for justice. These scenes broaden our view of biblical prayer: they suggest that prayer is not merely an earthly activity but resonates in the cosmic realm. However, deciding whether to categorize certain passages—like spontaneous acclamations of praise by heavenly multitudes—as "prayers" or "songs of worship" can be subjective.

4.2 Approaches to Number of Prayers

Given the breadth and variety of biblical texts, counting the number of prayers is more complex than it may initially appear. Different scholars and Bible students adopt different methodologies, each with its own rationale and potential pitfalls. Below are some of the main considerations that arise when attempting an enumeration.

4.2.1 Defining What Constitutes a "Prayer"

1. **Explicit vs. Implicit Prayers** Some texts clearly indicate prayer by using Hebrew or Greek terms like "pray," "entreat," "call upon," or "petition." However, others simply describe a person talking to God or hearing from Him without the narrative explicitly labeling it as prayer. For instance, if a prophet has a conversation with God that includes pleas or questions, do we count that entire dialogue as prayer? Or do we only count the portion where the prophet specifically addresses God with petition or praise? Additionally, certain exclamations might function as prayers in context. Peter's cry, "Lord, save me!" (Matthew 14:30), though brief, is obviously a plea to Jesus. Is that a "prayer," or more an instinctive outburst? Such distinctions affect the overall tally.

2. **Narrative Summaries** The Bible frequently summarizes events with phrases like "David inquired of the LORD" (1 Samuel 23:2, 4). Each "inquiry" presumably involved prayer, but the text does not always present David's exact words. If a single chapter states "David inquired of the LORD" multiple times, do we count each instance individually or collectively as one extended prayer? Scholars vary, with some adopting an inclusive approach—counting every mention of "inquiry," "calling upon the Lord," or "seeking God" as a distinct prayer—while others consider only fully narrated prayers.

3. **Poetic Sections** In the Psalms, for example, each psalm might be counted as a single prayer, or one might identify multiple prayerful units within certain psalms. Similarly, if a prophetic book includes an extended prayer of lament that spans multiple verses, do we count the entire section as one prayer, or do we partition it based on shifts in theme?

The biblical text does not typically label such segments with headings like "Prayer #1," "Prayer #2," so interpretive choices abound.

4. **Liturgical Forms** Certain biblical passages resemble liturgies or corporate blessings. The priestly blessing in Numbers 6:24–26, for instance, is often recited as a prayer over the people. Yet the text itself calls it a blessing or formula rather than a direct address to God. Does this constitute prayer, or is it a pronouncement over the people by God's command? Such borderline cases further complicate any attempt at a strict tally.

4.2.2 Recognizing Implicit vs. Explicit Prayers

As touched on above, the difference between explicit and implicit prayers is significant. **Explicit prayers** include clear indicators: a speaker addressing God by name, typical prayer language such as "O LORD," or words like "asked," "prayed," or "called out." **Implicit prayers**, on the other hand, involve dialogues with God or references to seeking God's will that do not label themselves as prayers. The Old Testament's phrase "inquired of the LORD" is the prime example, as are the many times characters "worship" or "bow down" but do not record the exact words spoken.

Those who adopt a *broader definition* of prayer—counting every instance in which people direct requests or worship toward God— arrive at significantly higher numbers. Others who prefer a *stricter definition* might limit their count to passages explicitly identified as prayers or that clearly follow a form of prayer (for instance, a personal address to God plus a petition or praise).

4.2.3 Tallying Old Testament vs. New Testament

Some have attempted to tally prayers separately in each Testament, discovering that the Old Testament contains a larger aggregate of references, partly because it covers a much longer historical period and includes the massive corpus of the Psalms. The New Testament, though shorter, is equally rich in spiritual content, featuring many prayers by Jesus, His disciples, and early church figures. However, the presence of multiple short prayers and references in the New Testament can inflate the count if each is enumerated individually.

1. **Variations in Language** The original languages—Hebrew in the Old Testament, Greek in the New Testament—use different terms for prayer. This language shift can influence how interpreters identify references. For instance, the Greek word *proseuchomai* (to pray) appears frequently in the New Testament. Similarly, the Hebrew Bible uses terms like *palal* (to intercede, pray) or phrases such as *qara' el-YHWH* (to call upon the LORD). Translators sometimes render these differently, adding complexity when readers attempt a direct word search in English Bibles.

2. **Literary Forms and Density** The Old Testament includes extensive narrative sections, wisdom literature, and large-scale histories that can embed prayers in the midst of genealogies, wars, and political developments. The New Testament, particularly the Epistles, includes many condensed references to prayer or short prayerful statements. Some readers may find it easier to locate and count these short statements than to comb through narrative sections like 1–2 Chronicles, where prayer references can slip into summarizing phrases.

4.2.4 Final Tally Challenges

Because of all the factors above, no universally agreed-upon count of the prayers in Scripture exists. Some commentators claim there are about 650 prayers in the Bible; others propose more than 700.

Still others arrive at a lower figure, citing closer to 300 or 400, depending on their methodology and definitions. Typically, the difference arises from whether:

- One includes every instance of "inquire of the LORD" or "call upon the LORD."

- One counts each psalm as a single prayer or divides it into multiple prayers.

- One includes short exclamations, blessings, or doxologies as separate prayers.

- One includes all references to worship or only those that explicitly address God.

While these numerical discrepancies might frustrate those seeking a single authoritative figure, they also highlight Scripture's depth and complexity. The act of attempting to count biblical prayers can itself become a devotional exercise, leading one to read the text more carefully, notice subtleties, and appreciate the tapestry of prayer that undergirds the biblical narrative.

4.3 Notable Examples

Rather than simply debate a final tally, many biblical interpreters prefer to highlight *examples* that illustrate the scope and variety of prayer in Scripture. Two categories often stand out: the shortest prayers and the longest prayers. Although these categories are somewhat arbitrary, they offer a glimpse into the breadth of expression that characterizes biblical prayer.

4.3.1 The Shortest Prayers in the Bible

1. **Peter's Plea: "Lord, save me!" (Matthew 14:30)** After stepping out of the boat to walk on water toward Jesus, Peter is overcome by fear when he sees the wind and

waves. He begins to sink and cries out, "Lord, save me!" This urgent, three-word plea often appears on lists of the Bible's shortest prayers. Though concise, it expresses desperation and faith—Peter recognizes Jesus as the one who can rescue him. This brief exclamation underlines that prayers need not be lengthy or formal to be genuine.

2. **The Tax Collector's Cry: "God, be merciful to me, a sinner!" (Luke 18:13)** Jesus's parable of the Pharisee and the tax collector contrasts self-righteousness with humble confession. The tax collector's prayer is a simple, heartfelt admission of guilt and plea for divine mercy. Jesus affirms that this short, unpretentious petition results in the tax collector "going home justified." Again, the entire prayer— "God, be merciful to me, a sinner!"—contains just a handful of words, yet it encapsulates repentance and dependence on God's grace.

3. **Jesus's Brief Prayers on the Cross** Even some of Jesus's utterances while crucified can be viewed as short prayers: "Father, forgive them, for they know not what they do" (Luke 23:34) and "Father, into your hands I commit my spirit!" (Luke 23:46). Although they are not exhaustive treatises, they directly address God, revealing the Son's trust and compassion in moments of excruciating anguish.

Each of these succinct prayers highlights that the *length* of a prayer does not dictate its significance or efficacy. Short prayers can pack profound spiritual content, offering a direct line to God in moments of crisis, confession, or praise.

4.3.2 The Longest Prayers in the Bible

1. **Solomon's Dedication of the Temple (1 Kings 8:22–53)** When Solomon completes the building of the Temple, he

gathers the people of Israel for a grand dedication ceremony. His prayer is extensive, covering themes of covenant faithfulness, the inevitability of sin, the hope of repentance, and God's willingness to forgive those who turn back to Him. This prayer occupies over thirty verses in 1 Kings 8. If included in the count, it would certainly rank among the longest formal prayers in Scripture. It is also repeated, with minor variations, in 2 Chronicles 6:14–42, illustrating how significant this moment was for Israel's national identity.

2. **Nehemiah's Confession for the Nation (Nehemiah 9:5–37)** Following the rebuilding of Jerusalem's walls, Nehemiah and the returned exiles gathered for a solemn assembly of repentance and covenant renewal. The Levites lead a lengthy prayer that recounts Israel's history, from Abraham's calling to the exiles' present plight. This prayer is notable not just for its length but for its sweeping theological scope—praising God's mercy, lamenting the people's repeated disobedience, and petitioning for restoration. Its fifty-plus verses (if one includes the invocation in verse 5) form one of the most detailed communal confessions in the Bible.

3. **Daniel's Intercessory Prayer (Daniel 9:4–19)** Though shorter than Solomon's and Nehemiah's prayers, Daniel 9 still ranks as one of the longer recorded prayers, focusing intently on confession and supplication. Daniel acknowledges the sins of his people, recognizes God's justice, and pleads for mercy on the basis of God's character rather than any merit of Israel. It stands as a paradigmatic prayer of repentance, cited often in discussions of biblical intercession. Whether one labels it "long" depends on the textual measure, but its intensity

and detail are substantial.

Such extended prayers, often called "set prayers" or "formal prayers," give theologians and lay readers alike a window into the communal and covenantal dimensions of biblical devotion. They convey theological truths—God's holiness, people's sinfulness, the hope of restoration—and underscore how prayer can incorporate historical remembrance and national repentance.

4.3.3 Other Exemplary Prayers

In addition to the extremes of very short and very long prayers, Scripture overflows with examples that illustrate diverse moods and circumstances. Here are just a few additional highlights relevant to the counting discussion:

- **Hannah's Prayer (1 Samuel 2:1–10)**: A profound song of thanksgiving that also serves as a theological reflection on God's sovereignty.

- **Hezekiah's Petition (2 Kings 19:14–19)**: A fervent appeal for deliverance from invading forces, showing how desperate situations inspire intense intercession.

- **The Lord's Prayer (Matthew 6:9–13; Luke 11:2–4)**: Often memorized and recited, it exemplifies a concise model prayer, though it was addressed at length in earlier chapters of this book under "How to Pray."

- **Jesus's High Priestly Prayer (John 17)**: A deeply personal intercession for the disciples and all believers, revealing Jesus's priorities on unity and sanctification.

Each of these can be counted as one prayer or dissected into multiple prayerful segments, depending on one's methodology and interpretive framework.

In conclusion, the Bible's numerous prayers, appearing in narratives, poetry, prophecy, and letters, attest that prayer is a driving force among God's people across centuries and cultures. While it is neither simple nor unanimous to pin down an exact tally of these prayers, the attempt to do so underscores their ubiquity and significance. Whether brief pleas for mercy or lengthy national confessions, each recorded prayer reveals another facet of humanity's relationship with God—our struggles, our hopes, our praises, our repentance. In this sense, the number of prayers in Scripture, whatever figure one arrives at, serves as a powerful testament to the transforming potential of communion with the Divine.

Chapter 5: People of Prayer (Who Prayed)

From Genesis to Revelation, the biblical narrative is filled with men and women who turn to God in moments of need, gratitude, confusion, or repentance. Some are prominent leaders—Abraham, Moses, David—who shape entire epochs of salvation history. Others are comparatively obscure, appearing for only a few verses yet leaving a testimony of earnest prayer. The New Testament then expands the circle, showcasing how Jesus Himself prays, how His disciples follow suit, and how ordinary believers—Jew and Gentile alike—discover the power of prayer in daily life and communal gatherings.

5.1 Key Old Testament Figures

The Old Testament covers an enormous span of history, from primordial times in Genesis through the centuries of Israel's monarchy and prophetic tradition. Amid that rich tapestry, certain individuals emerge as paradigmatic "people of prayer" whose examples echo through subsequent generations. Below, we survey some of the most notable: **Abraham** (intercession), **Moses** (pleas for Israel), **David** (psalms and supplications), as well as other significant voices like **Elijah**, **Hannah**, and **Daniel**.

5.1.1 Abraham's Intercessions

Abraham stands as one of the earliest and most iconic figures of prayer in Scripture. Although Genesis does not always frame his dialogues with God in explicit "prayer" terminology, the substance of his conversations displays the essence of heartfelt communion. One of the most striking examples occurs in Genesis 18:22–33, when Abraham pleads for the city of Sodom. Learning of the city's impending judgment, he boldly intercedes with God, asking whether the Lord would spare it for the sake of fifty righteous people, then forty-five, then forty, continuing down to ten.

1. **Intercession Rooted in God's Character** Abraham's repeated appeals hinge on God's justice and mercy. He asks, "Shall not the Judge of all the earth do what is just?" (Genesis 18:25). This rhetorical question underscores Abraham's understanding that God's righteousness governs divine actions. Intercession, therefore, emerges from a conviction that God *cares* about justice and mercy— a conviction that Abraham holds deeply.

2. **Boldness and Humility** Notably, Abraham recognizes his own unworthiness, describing himself as "dust and ashes" (Genesis 18:27). Yet he approaches God with remarkable boldness, pushing the boundaries of how many righteous people might suffice to avert judgment. This tension between humility and audacity characterizes biblical intercession, teaching later generations that effective prayer can be both reverent and persistent.

3. **Later Intercessions** In Genesis 20:7 and 17, Abraham again prays—this time for Abimelech, who unwittingly risked divine wrath by taking Sarah into his household. God

instructs Abimelech to have Abraham pray for him, highlighting Abraham's recognized role as an intercessor. That Abraham prays for a foreign king, one who nearly compromised his wife, further illustrates the breadth of his intercession. It is not limited to family or immediate circles; it extends to strangers and even adversaries under threat of God's judgment.

5.1.2 Moses's Pleas for Israel

If Abraham inaugurates the tradition of intercessory prayer, Moses takes it to new heights. Leading the Israelites out of Egypt, Moses continually stands between a rebellious nation and the holiness of God. Time and again, Scripture shows God expressing anger at Israel's disobedience, yet Moses "implores" or "pleads" for mercy.

1. **The Golden Calf Crisis** (Exodus 32) After receiving the Law on Mount Sinai, Moses descends to find the people worshiping a golden calf. God threatens destruction, offering to make a new nation from Moses alone. In Exodus 32:11–14, Moses intercedes passionately, appealing to God's reputation among the Egyptians ("Why should the Egyptians say…?") and reminding the Lord of His covenant promises to Abraham, Isaac, and Jacob. Remarkably, the text concludes with God "relenting" from the intended disaster. This does not suggest that God changes in His nature, but that Moses's intercession aligns with God's overarching plan of salvation and underscores the significance of covenant.

2. **Intercessory Dynamics** Moses's pleas highlight a pattern:

    o **Appealing to God's Character**: Moses calls on God's mercy, lovingkindness, and commitment to the patriarchs.

o **Identifying with the People**: Instead of distancing himself from Israel's sin, Moses stands in solidarity, even offering in Exodus 32:32 to have his own name blotted out if God will not forgive them.

o **Bold Honesty**: Moses sometimes prays for divine forgiveness while simultaneously acknowledging the seriousness of sin. His prayers balance a plea for compassion with respect for God's holiness.

3. **A Model for Spiritual Leadership** Across Exodus, Numbers, and Deuteronomy, Moses repeatedly demonstrates how leaders bear the burden of interceding for their communities. While he shares God's frustration at Israel's stubbornness (Numbers 11:10–15), he regularly steps into the breach, pleading for divine mercy. This selfless stance underscores that true spiritual leadership is grounded in prayerful concern for others, not merely administrative or political skill.

5.1.3 David's Psalms and Supplications

David's prayer life is immortalized in the Psalms, a substantial collection of songs and prayers that he either composed or inspired. While not every psalm is definitively traced to David, tradition and internal evidence affirm that many sprang from his experiences as shepherd, fugitive, king, and penitent sinner.

1. **Personal Relationship with God** When we think of David and prayer, the Book of Psalms naturally comes to mind. In these poems, David addresses God in first-person language, revealing an intimate bond. For instance, in Psalm 23 he celebrates the Lord as his Shepherd, guiding and protecting him. Psalm 51 records his repentance after the Bathsheba incident, illustrating how David's prayers

encompass both heartfelt remorse and trust in God's forgiveness.

2. **Seeking God's Guidance** Beyond the poetic texts, narratives in 1–2 Samuel show David "inquiring of the LORD" on critical matters. For example, in 1 Samuel 23:9–12, he seeks God's guidance about whether to engage the Philistines and whether certain townspeople would betray him. David's reliance on divine counsel shapes many of his military and political decisions, setting him apart from leaders who rely solely on human wisdom.

3. **Public Worship and National Leadership** As king, David oversaw the consolidation of Israel's worship in Jerusalem. In 2 Samuel 7:18–29, after hearing God's promise to establish his throne perpetually, David responds with a prayer of awe and gratitude. He marvels at God's generosity, proclaiming, "Who am I, O Lord GOD, and what is my house, that you have brought me thus far?" (2 Samuel 7:18). This prayer, combining humility and praise, forms a blueprint for how leaders can publicly honor God's faithfulness while acknowledging their own unworthiness.

4. **Legacy of the Psalms** David's prayers—especially in the Psalms—resonate throughout subsequent biblical history. They become the prayerbook of Israel and later Christianity, shaping the devotional life of believers. From lament (Psalm 22) to enthronement psalms (Psalm 24), from confession (Psalm 51) to thanksgiving (Psalm 138), David's prayers cover the full emotional range, teaching that *no* aspect of human experience is off-limits in approaching God.

5.1.4 Additional Old Testament Figures of Prayer

While Abraham, Moses, and David stand out, the Old Testament offers many other individuals who sought God in distinctive ways:

1. **Elijah and the Contest on Mount Carmel** (1 Kings 18:36–39) Elijah's showdown with the prophets of Baal culminates in a public prayer for fire from heaven. The brevity of his petition—seeking to prove that the LORD is God—emphasizes dependence on divine power. God's dramatic response vindicates Elijah's faith. Elijah's subsequent prayers also include pleas for rain after a prolonged drought (1 Kings 18:41–45) and even personal despair (1 Kings 19:4). Collectively, these episodes demonstrate how prayer can forge a prophet's courage while also revealing human frailty.

2. **Hannah's Petition for a Child** (1 Samuel 1:9–18; 2:1–10) Hannah's silent yet fervent prayer at the Tabernacle stands among the most moving depictions of personal petition in Scripture. Grieved by infertility and societal reproach, she pours out her heart so intensely that Eli the priest initially mistakes her for being drunk. God grants her a son, Samuel, whom she dedicates to the LORD. In gratitude, she composes a song of praise (1 Samuel 2:1–10) that foreshadows Mary's Magnificat in the New Testament.

3. **Daniel's Devotions and Intercession** (Daniel 6:10; 9:3–19) Daniel's commitment to prayer is evident: even under threat of death by lions, he maintains his threefold daily prayer routine (Daniel 6:10). Later, in Daniel 9:3–19, he offers a lengthy intercessory prayer on behalf of Israel, confessing national sins and appealing to God's mercy. Daniel's prayer weaves together historical reflection, confession, and a plea for restoration—illustrating that prayer can be deeply theological, informed by an awareness of God's unfolding plan.

4. **Hezekiah's Prayer for Deliverance** (2 Kings 19:14–19)
   Faced with the Assyrian threat under Sennacherib, King
   Hezekiah takes the enemy's threatening letter and literally
   spreads it before the LORD in the Temple. His prayer
   acknowledges God's sovereignty over all kingdoms,
   testifying that deliverance rests in God's hands alone.
   Shortly thereafter, the Assyrian forces suffer a devastating
   blow, underscoring the potency of earnest prayer in dire
   circumstances.

Collectively, these Old Testament figures remind us that prayer
took shape in many contexts—personal distress, national crisis,
public demonstrations of faith, or quiet devotion. Their stories
highlight that prayer is not a religious duty reserved for special
occasions but the heartbeat of a life oriented toward God's
covenant promises.

5.2 Major New Testament Voices

The advent of Jesus the Messiah ushers in the New Testament era,
where prayer remains central but takes on new dimensions in light
of the Incarnation and the birth of the Church. This section
spotlights two major categories of New Testament "people of
prayer": **Jesus Himself** and **His followers** (the apostles and the early
church).

5.2.1 Jesus: The Perfect Model of Prayer

Biblical References: Matthew 14:23; Mark 1:35; Luke 5:16; Luke
6:12; John 17

No single figure in Scripture embodies prayer more fully than Jesus.
As the eternal Son of God, He nonetheless lived on earth in
dependence on the Father, modeling consistent communion with
God. While Chapter 2 has explored *how* Jesus taught His disciples
to pray (e.g., the Lord's Prayer in Matthew 6:9–13), here we focus

on *who* He was as one who prayed.

1. **Frequent Withdrawal to Solitude** The Synoptic Gospels (Matthew, Mark, Luke) repeatedly note that Jesus withdrew to lonely places to pray. Mark 1:35 shows Him rising "very early in the morning" to find solitude before beginning His ministry tasks. Luke 6:12 describes Him spending an entire night in prayer prior to selecting the Twelve. These accounts underscore prayer as integral to His ministry decisions and spiritual renewal.

2. **Intimacy with the Father** Jesus addressed God as "Father," conveying a relationship of love, trust, and submission. In John 17, known as the High Priestly Prayer, He prays for Himself (that the Father would glorify Him), for His disciples (that they would be sanctified and unified), and for future believers (that they, too, would experience oneness with Him and the Father). This remarkable prayer reveals the depth of Christ's concern for His Church across time and emphasizes that divine fellowship fuels intercession.

3. **Prayers in Public and Private Moments**

    o   **Public Thanksgiving**: Jesus gave thanks before feeding the multitudes (Matthew 14:19) and publicly thanked the Father for hearing His prayer at Lazarus's tomb (John 11:41–42).

    o   **Prayer in Anguish**: In Gethsemane, Jesus's earnest prayer highlights emotional agony as He wrestles with the looming crucifixion (Matthew 26:36–44; Mark 14:32–39). He ultimately surrenders to the Father's will.

    o   **Prayer on the Cross**: Even during crucifixion, Jesus prays, "Father, forgive them..." (Luke 23:34) and later commits His spirit to God (Luke 23:46). These moments affirm that no circumstance is too dire for prayer.

4. **Legacy for Believers** Jesus not only *taught* prayer but *exemplified* it, forging a path for disciples to approach God with confidence. His own prayer life underscores that prayer is not a peripheral activity but the lifeblood of a relationship with the Father. This example profoundly shaped the apostles and early church believers who followed.

5.2.2 The Apostles and the Early Church

After Jesus's ascension, His disciples remained steadfast in prayer, seeking the Holy Spirit's guidance and power. The Book of Acts provides a historical window into how prayer sustained the early Christian community, while the Epistles reveal the apostles' ongoing dedication to intercession and thanksgiving.

1. **Prayer at the Church's Birth** (Acts 1–2) The small band of believers, numbering around 120, devoted themselves to prayer (Acts 1:14). Before the Holy Spirit's arrival at Pentecost, they gathered in the upper room, unified in seeking God's promise. This posture of expectancy underscores that the outpouring of the Spirit did not occur in a vacuum. It happened to a praying community. Acts 2:42 then summarizes the nascent church's key practices: "They devoted themselves to the apostles' teaching and the fellowship, to the breaking of bread and *the prayers.*"

2. **Apostolic Leadership in Prayer**

   o **Peter and John**: After being threatened by the Jewish council (Acts 4:23–31), they join the believers in a communal prayer that acknowledges

God's sovereignty and asks for boldness in preaching. The place is shaken, symbolizing divine affirmation.

- o **Paul**: Though initially a persecutor, once converted, Paul's life becomes saturated with prayer. Acts 9:11 suggests that when he was blinded, he was found praying. Throughout his letters, he prays for the churches (Romans 1:9–10; Ephesians 1:15–19; Philippians 1:3–4), and he urges believers to pray continually (1 Thessalonians 5:17). Paul's prayers often blend thanksgiving, intercession, and teaching about God's grace, displaying a theology robustly shaped by communion with the risen Christ.

- o **James and Other Apostles**: James, the brother of Jesus, famously taught about prayer in James 5:13–18, highlighting the prayer of faith and the example of Elijah. Although James was not part of the original Twelve, tradition and Scripture portray him as a leader in the Jerusalem church and a man of prayer who called on believers to intercede for the sick.

3. **Communal and Missional Prayer** Acts demonstrates that the early church's mission—spreading the gospel beyond Jewish contexts—was fueled by united intercession. When Peter was imprisoned by Herod, "earnest prayer for him was made to God by the church" (Acts 12:5). Shortly thereafter, an angel miraculously frees him. Similarly, in Acts 13:1–3, leaders in the Antioch church fast and pray before commissioning Barnabas and Paul for missionary work. Such episodes underscore that corporate prayer shaped the church's decisions and catalyzed missionary

endeavors.

4. **Prayer as a Hallmark of Faith** In sum, the New Testament church exemplifies that the *who* of prayer encompasses everyone—from apostles to lay members. The readiness to pray, whether in private homes or in temple courts, in times of persecution or joy, reveals prayer's integral role in shaping the Church's character and growth.

5.3 Ordinary Individuals and Groups

While the Bible highlights monumental figures like Abraham, Moses, David, or Paul, it also pays attention to everyday people whose prayers may appear in only a few verses, yet teach profound lessons. In this section, we explore two categories that underscore the breadth of "who prayed" in Scripture: **women of prayer** who often broke cultural boundaries, and **Gentiles and outsiders** who were drawn into God's grace through earnest seeking. Each reveals that prayer is not reserved for religious elites or those of a particular ethnicity or status, but extends to all who approach the Lord in faith.

5.3.1 Women of Prayer

Throughout both the Old and New Testaments, women display remarkable devotion through prayer, challenging cultural norms that often diminished their public religious roles. We have already mentioned Hannah, but other notable examples abound:

1. **Hagar (Genesis 16:7–13; 21:15–19)** Although Hagar's direct addresses to God are limited, the narratives show God hearing her cry in the wilderness. In Genesis 16, pregnant and mistreated by Sarai, Hagar flees and encounters "the angel of the LORD," who promises to bless her offspring. Hagar responds by naming the LORD "El Roi"—the God who sees me. In Genesis 21, again cast out, Hagar despairs as

water runs out. God hears the boy Ishmael's cries and shows Hagar a well. Though these passages do not record lengthy prayers from Hagar's lips, her plight and God's compassionate response underscore that even marginalized figures experience divine care.

2. **Ruth's Loyalty and Naomi's Blessing (Ruth 1:16–17; 2:12)** While the Book of Ruth does not feature extended formal prayers by Ruth herself, her famous declaration of loyalty to Naomi—"Your people shall be my people, and your God my God" (Ruth 1:16)—foreshadows a trust in the LORD that forms the basis of her faith. Meanwhile, Naomi repeatedly invokes divine blessing upon Boaz and her daughter-in-law (Ruth 2:19–20; 3:1). These short benedictions highlight how ordinary women in everyday settings—gleaning fields, family relationships—invoke God's favor, bridging daily life and spiritual devotion.

3. **Deborah and Miriam in Worshipful Prayer-Song** Deborah, a judge and prophetess, composes a victory song with Barak after defeating Canaanite oppression (Judges 5). This poetic expression, though largely recounting the battle, is directed in thanks to God, effectively functioning as prayerful praise. Miriam, sister of Moses, similarly leads Israelite women in a song of triumph after the Red Sea crossing (Exodus 15:20–21). Their leadership in corporate worship underscores how women also played central roles in Israel's spiritual life.

4. **Anna (Luke 2:36–38)** Transitioning to the New Testament, Anna, an elderly prophetess, provides a poignant picture of lifelong devotion. A widow for many decades, she "did not depart from the temple, worshiping with fasting and prayer night and day" (Luke 2:37). When she encounters the infant Jesus, she recognizes Him as the long-awaited Messiah and

gives thanks to God, speaking about the child to all who awaited Jerusalem's redemption. Anna's fidelity in prayer becomes a model of patient, hopeful intercession culminating in joyous recognition of God's promise fulfilled.

5. **Mary, Mother of Jesus** Mary's prayers are glimpsed in her responses to angelic revelation and the "Magnificat" (Luke 1:46–55), which, although a hymn of praise, is also an intimate address to God. Her example stands as one of humble submission: "Behold, I am the servant of the Lord; let it be to me according to your word" (Luke 1:38). This posture, though not a formal petition, exhibits a heart open to God's purposes—an implicit prayer of acceptance that resonates through Christian tradition.

Through these diverse portraits—Hagar the outcast, Deborah the judge, Anna the prophetess, Mary the mother of Jesus—Scripture honors women who turn to God in faith, whether in crisis or celebration. Their prayers and praises reflect God's inclusive love, welcoming the voices of those whom society often overlooked.

5.3.2 Gentiles and Outsiders Who Called on God

From the Old Testament's inclusive glimpses to the New Testament's explicit commission to "make disciples of all nations" (Matthew 28:19), the Bible affirms that God's compassion transcends ethnic and social boundaries. Several accounts demonstrate that even "outsiders"—foreigners, Gentiles, or those deemed unclean—can pray to the living God and be heard.

1. **Naaman the Syrian (2 Kings 5)** Naaman, a high-ranking Aramean commander stricken with leprosy, seeks healing from the God of Israel after hearing from his wife's Israelite servant girl. Although the text does not record a formal prayer by Naaman, his actions reflect seeking God's help

through Elisha the prophet. His eventual healing and declaration—"Behold, I know that there is no God in all the earth but in Israel" (2 Kings 5:15)—suggest a turning of heart. While primarily a miracle story, the narrative underlines that a Gentile's sincere approach to God does not go unanswered.

2. **The Ninevites (Book of Jonah)** Jonah's reluctant mission to Nineveh brings about a sweeping revival: the pagan inhabitants, from king to commoner, repent in sackcloth and ashes (Jonah 3:5–9). Though their prayers are not scripted in detail, they collectively "call out mightily to God" (Jonah 3:8), and God responds by sparing them. This underscores that genuine humility, even among those outside Israel's covenant community, can elicit divine mercy.

3. **Roman Centurion Cornelius (Acts 10)** In the New Testament, Cornelius emerges as a pivotal figure in the early Church's expansion beyond Jewish boundaries. Described as "a devout man who feared God... [and who] prayed continually" (Acts 10:2), Cornelius receives an angelic vision instructing him to send for Peter. This leads to the famous "Gentile Pentecost," where the Holy Spirit falls upon Cornelius's household (Acts 10:44–48). Cornelius's prayers, though not preserved verbatim, clearly ascend to God, who orchestrates a monumental shift in the Church's mission—accepting Gentiles without requiring them to become Jewish proselytes first.

4. **The Syrophoenician (Canaanite) Woman (Matthew 15:21–28; Mark 7:24–30)** This unnamed Gentile woman begs Jesus to deliver her daughter from a demon. Though initially rebuffed (Jesus references the focus of His mission on "the lost sheep of the house of Israel"), she persists,

humbly accepting her "outsider" status yet boldly asserting her right to divine mercy. Jesus commends her faith and grants her request. Her insistent plea, "Have mercy on me, O Lord, Son of David," stands as a powerful example of fervent supplication from beyond Israel's ethnic boundaries.

5. **The Ethiopian Eunuch (Acts 8:26–39)** While not explicitly described as "praying," this official from Ethiopia is found reading Isaiah's prophecy about the suffering servant. Philip the evangelist, guided by the Spirit, explains the Scripture to him. The eunuch's eagerness to understand and his immediate desire for baptism reveal a receptive heart, akin to prayerful openness. This story again underlines God's readiness to embrace those often deemed outsiders—whether due to ethnicity, physical condition, or cultural distance from Judaism.

In each of these cases, outsiders and Gentiles approach God or are approached by divine grace. Their stories confirm a grand biblical theme: that "everyone who calls on the name of the Lord shall be saved" (Joel 2:32; Romans 10:13). The "who" of prayer thus spans far beyond Israel's borders, foreshadowing the global reach of the gospel.

5.4 Extended Reflections: The Scope of "Who Prayed"

Having surveyed Old and New Testament exemplars—ranging from patriarchs and kings to prophets, apostles, women, and foreigners—we can draw several key insights into "who prayed" in the Bible:

1. **Prayer is Not Limited by Status or Title** Some of the greatest prayers come from kings and prophets (like David or Elijah), but Scripture also extols prayers from barren women, outcasts, and Gentiles. These narratives suggest

that the inclination to pray arises from human need, faith, or gratitude, cutting across distinctions of social rank, wealth, or cultural acceptance.

2. **Intercession as a Common Thread** Many biblical figures intercede for others—Abraham for Sodom, Moses for Israel, Daniel for his exiled people, and Paul for the churches. This repeated pattern underscores prayer's communal dimension: those who pray often stand as mediators, appealing to God for the benefit of broader communities, families, or even enemies. Indeed, such intercession becomes a hallmark of spiritual maturity and leadership in the biblical record.

3. **Diverse Motivations and Circumstances** People pray for deliverance from danger (Hezekiah, Jehoshaphat), for personal vindication (Hannah), for forgiveness and restoration (Nehemiah, David), for wisdom (Solomon), for blessings on others (Naomi), or simply to praise and worship (Deborah, Mary). This variety testifies that prayer engages every aspect of life—spiritual, emotional, ethical, and even political.

4. **God's Universal Invitation** The examples of Gentiles—Cornelius, the Syrophoenician woman, the Ninevites—demonstrate that even those outside the covenant community or early church membership can call upon the one true God. Their acceptance by God anticipates the New Testament's emphasis on global evangelism and the inclusion of all peoples. These stories encourage believers to realize that no one is beyond the reach of prayer or God's mercy.

5. **Ongoing Legacy in the Church** The Bible's portrayal of "people of prayer" shapes Christian understanding

throughout history. Saints and ordinary believers alike look to these examples for inspiration, seeing in biblical characters reflections of their own struggles and hopes. Prayer, therefore, is not an abstraction but a living tradition anchored in countless personal stories.

Chapter 6: Moments of Prayer (When Did They Pray)

6.1 Historical Context

Throughout the Old Testament, the unfolding story of Israel's relationship with God provides a broad historical canvas for understanding *when* prayer arose. From the earliest patriarchs living in a semi-nomadic culture, through the monarchy's consolidation of power, and into the prophetic calls for national repentance, prayer emerges in dramatic moments that alter individual destinies and national trajectories alike. In this section, we examine prayer *within* two overarching contexts: (1) the Patriarchal Era, and (2) the Monarchy and Prophetic Era.

6.1.1 Prayer in the Patriarchal Era

1. **Early Altars and Calls Upon the Name of the LORD** The biblical record often portrays the patriarchs—Abraham, Isaac, and Jacob—building altars as they traverse Canaan. When Scripture says they "called upon the name of the LORD," it describes an act of worship or petition that took

place at these altars (Genesis 12:7–8, 13:4, 26:25). While it may be tempting to view these events as routine religious rituals, the narratives suggest *significant turning points* that prompted prayer:

- o **Abraham's Journeys:** Each time Abraham settled in a new region, he built an altar. This marked not only the physical claim of God's promise ("I will give you this land," Genesis 12:7) but also Abraham's recognition that he needed divine favor and guidance to navigate an unknown territory. These altar-building moments functioned as both worship and entreaty: "We are here, God; remember Your covenant with us."

- o **Isaac Re-digging Wells:** Genesis 26 narrates how Isaac reopened wells originally dug by Abraham but seized by the Philistines. After each success, Isaac often called on the LORD for continued blessing and peace. These prayers were tethered to specific moments of conflict resolution or the reestablishment of boundaries.

2. **Covenant Episodes as Catalysts for Prayer** The patriarchal narratives hinge on covenants made or reaffirmed with Abraham, Isaac, and Jacob (Genesis 15, 17, 26:2–5, 28:10–22, 35:9–15). Whenever God restates the promise of land and descendants, or whenever a patriarch responds with faith, a moment of prayer emerges:

- o **Abraham's Dialogue over Sodom** (Genesis 18:22–33): This conversation, which can be classified as intercessory prayer, takes place just after a covenantal reaffirmation (Genesis 17). Abraham's bold "negotiation" is driven by God's revealed plan for the region, and the unique timing—right after Abraham has again heard of God's promises—underscores how prayer is often prompted by new or clarifying revelations of God's purpose.

- o **Jacob at Bethel** (Genesis 28:10–22): Fleeing his brother Esau, Jacob encounters God in a dream. He responds with a vow (Genesis 28:20–22) and a memorial pillar—both acts that revolve around seeking protection and pledging fidelity. Here, a divine revelation triggers Jacob's prayerful commitment, tying a significant life transition (leaving his family) to a fresh reliance on God.

3. **Moments of Personal Crisis and Transition** In patriarchal times, crises like famine, barrenness, family disputes, or threats from neighboring peoples sparked moments of prayer. For instance, *barrenness* is a recurring trial for the matriarchs:

- o **Rebekah's Barrenness**: Genesis 25:21 states Isaac prayed to the LORD for his wife because she was barren; the LORD granted his prayer, resulting in the birth of Esau and Jacob. This moment underscores how personal family crises drive patriarchs to entreat God for intervention.

- o **Jacob Wrestling at the Jabbok** (Genesis 32:22–32): On the eve of reuniting with Esau (whom he had deceived years prior), Jacob experiences a mysterious encounter—he "wrestles" with a man (implicitly representing God's angel). While this isn't labeled a traditional "prayer," it constitutes a nocturnal struggle that ends in blessing. The text suggests it was a turning point, a prayerful confrontation in which Jacob receives a new name, Israel ("he struggles with God"). This crucial transition from trickster to covenant heir is sealed through an all-night vigil that merges physical and spiritual striving.

4. **Job: A Paragon of Patriarchal Piety** Although its exact date is debated, the Book of Job may well reflect patriarchal-era faith. Job routinely offers burnt offerings on behalf of his children (Job 1:5), linking familial intercession to daily life. Later, amid his profound suffering, Job laments, petitions, and questions God in extended poetic discourses. These culminating dialogues (Job 38–42) can be viewed as a protracted moment of prayerful wrestling, akin to Jacob's experience. Although the speeches are not short formal prayers, the entire storyline orbits the question of how a righteous man prays in undeserved suffering. In the end, God vindicates Job's sincerity, again confirming that crisis moments in the patriarchal era often became occasions for deep communion with the Divine.

6.1.2 Prayer During the Monarchy and Prophetic Era

With the establishment of a monarchy in Israel (starting with Saul, then David, Solomon, and subsequent kings), Israel's religious life became more centralized. The Temple in Jerusalem became a focal point for worship and prayer, and prophets played an increasingly pivotal role in calling kings and people to righteousness. Each new era or event—such as coronations, temple dedications, wars, exiles—often spurred public or personal prayers.

1. **Coronations and National Events**

   o **Hannah's Prayer Leading to Samuel's Role** (1 Samuel 1–2): Though we do not repeat Hannah's story in depth (Chapter 5 touched on "who prayed"), her petition and subsequent thanksgiving are directly tied to national leadership transitions. Samuel, the child she prayed for, inaugurates Israel's move from tribal judges to monarchical governance. Thus, a single mother's prayer shapes the national trajectory.

- o **Saul's Anointing** (1 Samuel 10–12): While the text records more of Samuel's addresses than formal prayers at Saul's coronation, 1 Samuel 12:23 includes Samuel's promise: "far be it from me that I should sin against the LORD by ceasing to pray for you." This vow underscores that transitions in political leadership were prime moments for sustained intercession.

2. Temple Ceremonies and Covenant Renewals

- o **David's Preparatory Prayers**: David spent much of his reign planning for the Temple that his son Solomon would eventually build (1 Chronicles 22–29). Although David was barred from constructing it due to his wartime history (1 Chronicles 22:7–8), he prayed extensively for God's blessing on the project and on Solomon's leadership (1 Chronicles 29:10–20). These prayers coincide with national gatherings where leaders dedicated resources to the Temple's future.

- o **Solomon's Dedication Prayer** (1 Kings 8; 2 Chronicles 6): Possibly one of the grandest recorded prayers, Solomon's petition dedicating the new Temple weaves together pleas for forgiveness, blessing, and divine presence. The prayer specifically addresses hypothetical future moments: *when* Israel sins and is exiled, *when* foreigners pray toward this place, *when* famine or plague arises. Each scenario includes an appeal for God to hear from heaven. Thus, a single ceremonial moment (the Temple dedication) anticipates *many future moments* of crisis or gratitude that would prompt prayer in or toward the Temple.

o **Covenant Renewals**: Kings like Hezekiah and Josiah led major covenant-renewal ceremonies, which included prayer, repentance, and communal worship (2 Kings 18:1–7; 23:1–3; 2 Chronicles 29:20–30). These ceremonies typically followed times of national decline, idolatry, or invasion, reinforcing how a crisis or a new religious awakening triggered extended public prayer.

3. **Prophetic Confrontations and National Crises**

o **Elijah's Prayers in Drought and Showdown** (1 Kings 17–18): Elijah's era was rife with idolatry under King Ahab and Queen Jezebel. God withheld rain, and Elijah prayed first for sustenance (1 Kings 17:20–24) and later for rain's return (1 Kings 18:41–46). Most famously, he prayed at Mount Carmel for God to reveal Himself by fire (1 Kings 18:36–39). Each prayer coincided with a dramatic demonstration of God's power, illustrating how crisis-laden times in the monarchy often featured intense prophetic intercession.

o **Isaiah, Jeremiah, and Others**: Some prophets prayed for mercy on the nation (e.g., Isaiah's laments in Isaiah 63:15–64:12), while others, like

Jeremiah, were forbidden at times to intercede (Jeremiah 7:16) because of the people's obstinate sin. These moments highlight an evolving tension: as Israel's rebellion grew, the *when* of prayer often pivoted from pleas for deliverance to urgent calls for repentance or warnings of impending judgment.

o **Daniel in Exile** (Daniel 9): Although Daniel's story unfolds during the Babylonian and Persian reigns, his practices hearken back to the monarchy's historical context. He prays at set times even when forbidden (Daniel 6:10) and later offers a lengthy prayer of national confession (Daniel 9:3–19). Significantly, he prays upon realizing that Jeremiah's prophecy of a seventy-year exile was nearing completion (Daniel 9:2). Thus, the *moment*—a scriptural revelation about timing—compels Daniel to intensify his supplication, bridging the exilic era to the postexilic hope of returning to the land.

6.2 Praying in Crisis and Transition

While the historical overview above underscores that transitions in leadership or religious life spurred prayer, Scripture also provides ample examples of *personal* and *national* crises that prompt fervent appeal to God. This section focuses on two major categories: (1) deliverance from enemies, and (2) times of collective or national repentance. By examining these moments, we see prayer as a consistent response not only to hopeful new beginnings (like a king's coronation) but also to existential threats that drive people to their knees.

6.2.1 Deliverance from Enemies

Moses at the Red Sea (Exodus 14:10–14) One of the most iconic crisis prayers in Scripture occurs when the Israelites, newly freed from Egypt, find themselves trapped between the Red Sea and Pharaoh's approaching army. Although Moses's words to the people in Exodus 14:13–14 are presented more as a reassurance than a formal "prayer," verse 15 suggests Moses was crying out to God, to which the LORD replies, "Why do you cry to me? Tell the people of Israel to go forward." This brief but critical exchange underscores that *in the face of imminent destruction*, the leader's immediate reflex was to appeal to God's protection and guidance.

Samuel and the Philistine Threat (1 Samuel 7:5–14) Years after the conquest, during the judges' period bridging to the monarchy, the Philistines posed a constant menace. When the people gathered at Mizpah for repentance, the Philistines seized the opportunity to attack. Samuel offered a burnt offering and cried to the LORD (1 Samuel 7:9). God's intervention—thunder that discomfits the Philistines—testifies that *the very moment of enemy aggression* ignites fervent intercession, leading to decisive victory.

Hezekiah's Appeal Against Assyria (2 Kings 19:14–19; Isaiah 37:14–20) In the monarchy era, the Assyrian Empire threatened Judah under King Hezekiah. The besieging commander, Sennacherib's Rabshakeh, taunted the people, questioning God's ability to save. Hezekiah responded by spreading Sennacherib's threatening letter before God in the Temple and praying for deliverance. The event dramatizes how *external aggression* often sparked immediate, whole-hearted pleas for rescue. Shortly after, an angel of the LORD decimates the Assyrian camp (2 Kings 19:35).

Jehoshaphat's Confession of Helplessness (2 Chronicles 20:1–30) Another vivid narrative is the coalition of Moabites, Ammonites, and Meunites marching against Judah under King Jehoshaphat. The king calls a national assembly at the Temple, declaring, "We do not know what to do, but our eyes are on you" (2 Chronicles 20:12).

This simple prayer of dependence exemplifies the posture that crisis can evoke: acknowledging one's utter inability to stand without God's aid. The subsequent miraculous victory—fought more by divine ambush than Judah's military strength—reinforces the biblical theme that God responds powerfully to genuine pleas for help.

David's Hymns of Deliverance (Psalm 18, among others) David's psalms repeatedly mention enemies and persecutors. While these references can be spiritual (metaphorical foes like temptation) or personal (Saul, Absalom, foreign adversaries), David frames deliverance as a response to prayer. Psalm 18, for instance, is David's song of gratitude after God rescues him from Saul. The psalm's structure includes David calling upon the LORD in distress (vv. 4–6), God's majestic intervention (vv. 7–15), and the final celebration of deliverance (vv. 16–50). This poem reaffirms that *the moment of dire threat* becomes an impetus for fervent supplication and eventual praise.

These examples across eras—Exodus, Judges/early monarchy, Davidic psalms, late monarchy—demonstrate a consistent pattern: *When enemies loom large*, biblical figures present desperate petitions for divine intervention, often culminating in decisive acts of salvation that reaffirm God's sovereignty.

6.2.2 Times of National Repentance

Cycle of Repentance in Judges The Book of Judges is structured around repeated cycles: Israel sins (usually idolatry), enemies oppress them, they cry out to the LORD, and God raises a deliverer (Judges 2:11–19). Although the text sometimes summarizes the "cry" without quoting lengthy prayers, these communal outcries represent crucial moments of repentance. At each juncture, the nation's realization of guilt or desperation triggers a renewed appeal for help.

Samuel's Mizpah Gathering (Revisited) As noted above, 1 Samuel 7 merges deliverance from the Philistines with national repentance. The people gather to confess, "We have sinned against the LORD" (1 Samuel 7:6). Samuel prays and offers sacrifices, bridging communal repentance with God's rescue. This synergy between *turning from sin* and *seeking divine mercy* reappears throughout Israel's history.

Post-Exilic Repentance in Nehemiah 9 After returning from Babylonian captivity, a portion of the Jewish community, led by Ezra and Nehemiah, rededicates itself to the covenant. Nehemiah 9:1–3 records how the people assemble in sackcloth, fasting, and confessing their sins. This solemn gathering includes an extended prayer (Nehemiah 9:5–37) rehearsing Israel's history of rebellion, God's forbearance, and the current desire for renewed obedience. The entire event is triggered by reading the Law (Nehemiah 8) and recognizing how far they had strayed. Thus, a rediscovery of God's Word in a moment of communal reflection sparks contrition and extended intercession.

Prophetic Calls for National Lament

- o **Joel's Appeal** (Joel 1:13–14; 2:12–17): Facing a catastrophic locust plague, the prophet Joel instructs priests to "put on sackcloth" and to gather elders and inhabitants for a sacred assembly of fasting and weeping. "Return to me with all your heart," God exhorts (Joel 2:12). These calls highlight how natural disasters or national calamities prompt official gatherings for lamentation, confession, and pleas for restoration.

- o **Jonah and Nineveh**: Though Nineveh is a foreign city, its mass repentance (Jonah 3:5–9) exemplifies how crisis (the threat of destruction) leads to widespread fasting and prayer. While not Israelite, the Ninevites' example stands parallel to Israel's own patterns, further illustrating the universal impetus of *moment-driven* repentance.

Collectively, these events underscore that national repentance is frequently catalyzed by *recognition of sin*, a reading or revelation of God's Word, or crises that expose spiritual decay. In each scenario, *the moment of realization or threat* fosters communal gatherings, confession, and prayer, often culminating in renewed covenant commitment and divine reprieve.

6.3 Praying in Worship and Celebration

Not all biblical prayer arises from crisis or serious transitions. Scripture equally depicts prayer in contexts of joyful worship, praise, and communal festivals. This section explores how *victories*, *festivals*, and *liturgical gatherings* become occasions for uplifting prayers—distinct from the supplication and repentance that typically characterize crisis prayer.

6.3.1 Festival Gatherings and Holy Days

Established Feasts in the Torah The Mosaic Law designates several feasts—Passover, the Feast of Weeks (Pentecost), the Feast of Booths (Tabernacles), and so forth (Leviticus 23; Deuteronomy 16). Although these chapters often focus on sacrifices and offerings, prayer was implicitly intertwined with these observances. For instance:

o **Passover Commemoration**: Each year, families recounted the Exodus story, giving thanks for divine deliverance. While the text does not record formal prayers repeated annually, the retelling of the Exodus and the worship around Passover inherently involve praising God for salvation. Over time, Jewish tradition developed liturgical blessings and psalms (the "Hallel," Psalms 113–118) that believers recited during Passover, transforming these days into *prayerful* communal remembrances.

o **Feast of Tabernacles**: As a harvest festival and commemoration of wilderness wanderings, this feast blended gratitude for agricultural blessings with recollections of God's guidance (Deuteronomy 16:13–15). Participants would dwell in temporary shelters (booths) to remember their ancestors' sojourn. Prayers of thanksgiving for the harvest and for God's faithful provision naturally punctuated the festival. Although the Torah does not specify a formal "prayer text" for the feast, the biblical emphasis on rejoicing before the LORD (Leviticus 23:40) underscores that corporate worship with petitions and thanks was integral.

Celebration after Temple Construction Beyond the well-known dedication prayer by Solomon (1 Kings 8), 2 Chronicles 5–7 recounts the celebratory aspect that accompanied the ark's installation in the Temple. The priests, Levites, and assembled Israelites sang praises, played instruments, and declared God's goodness (2 Chronicles 5:13). Fire from heaven's sign (2 Chronicles 7:1) further ignited worship, culminating in extended sacrifices, feasting, and presumably many prayers of joyful adoration. This "moment" was not just a short ceremony; it stretched into a festival that exemplified a *national outpouring of gratitude*.

Post-Exilic Festival Restorations After the exile, the returned community zealously revived their national feasts. Ezra 3:4–5 describes how they resumed the Feast of Booths even before the Temple was rebuilt, offering daily burnt offerings "as each day required." While the text focuses on sacrifices, it is inconceivable that prayer was absent during these newly reinstituted celebrations. Such gatherings combined the sorrow of exile's memory with the joy of restoration, culminating in a layered expression of worship that merged lament, praise, hope, and thanksgiving.

Zechariah's Vision for Joyful Feasts In Zechariah 8:19, God promises that the fast days commemorating Jerusalem's destruction would become "seasons of joy and gladness and cheerful feasts." This prophecy hints at a shift in *why* and *when* people prayed—from mourning their national tragedies to rejoicing in renewed covenant blessings. Thus, even once-somber days could transform into moments of celebratory prayer if the community responded to God's redemptive work.

Collectively, these festival contexts reveal that *holy days and communal feasts* were not merely times of ritual but also of spontaneous and corporate prayer—expressions of gratitude, wonder, and communal identity before the LORD.

6.3.2 Temple and Synagogue Worship

Temple as a House of Prayer King Solomon's dedication prayer explicitly portrays the Temple as a place where God's people (and even foreigners) would direct their prayers (1 Kings 8:30, 41–43). Throughout the monarchy and into the Second Temple period, worshipers traveled to Jerusalem, particularly during major feasts. Many biblical psalms—often called "Psalms of Ascent" (Psalms 120–134)—are believed to have been sung by pilgrims ascending to Jerusalem's heights. Psalm 122:1 exclaims, "I was glad when they said to me, 'Let us go to the house of the LORD!'" Such texts highlight that simply journeying to the Temple was an act of devotion culminating in prayerful worship upon arrival.

Daily Incense and Prayer Times

- o **In the Old Testament**: Priests offered incense on the altar of incense in the Holy Place twice daily (Exodus 30:7–8), morning and evening, symbolizing the prayers of the people rising to God (Psalm 141:2). While worshipers stood outside, they might offer silent or spoken prayers, trusting the priestly mediation.

- o **In the New Testament**: Luke 1:8–10 sets the scene where Zechariah, John the Baptist's father, is chosen to burn incense in the Temple. The people "were praying outside" during this moment. Thus, the ritual moment of incense burning coincided with communal prayer, blending personal petitions and the nation's worshipful stance. Luke specifically emphasizes that *all* assembled worshipers participated in prayer during the priest's service, confirming the Temple's role as a communal prayer hub.

Synagogue Gatherings After the exile, and especially in the intertestamental period, local synagogues emerged as centers for Scripture reading, teaching, and prayer. While the Old Testament does not detail synagogue practices, the New Testament Gospels depict Jesus reading Scripture in synagogues (Luke 4:16–20). The Book of Acts frequently portrays Paul preaching or engaging with Jewish communities in synagogues (Acts 13:14–15; 17:1–3). Though the narratives focus on teaching rather than formal prayer liturgies, the synagogue services included blessings, the Shema, and petitions, forming an additional moment for communal devotion.

Widows and Devout Individuals in God's House Figures like Anna (Luke 2:36–37) demonstrate that some devout believers worshiped "with fasting and prayer night and day" in the Temple precincts, turning the building into a near-continuous site of petition and praise. This indicates that the Temple was not solely for large-scale festivals or official sacrifices; it also served as a sanctuary for personal devotion at any hour.

Hence, the Temple and later synagogue gatherings provided a structured framework for the entire community's prayer life—whether at daily, weekly, or seasonal intervals. From priestly offerings to the laity's personal devotion, these institutions anchored prayer in an ongoing cycle of worship.

6.4 Extended Reflections on "When Did They Pray?" in a Biblical-Historical Sense

Having examined *historical contexts, crisis and transition*, and *times of worshipful celebration*, we observe that prayer in Scripture is not confined to daily rhythms (addressed in Chapter 3) but also surges forth at *turning points* in Israel's corporate and personal stories. Below are overarching reflections that tie these findings together:

1. **Prayer Is Tethered to Covenant Moments** Whether in the patriarchal era (Abraham's altar-building) or monarchy era (Solomon's Temple dedication), renewed or inaugurated covenants commonly spurred prayer. Because Israel's identity was so intertwined with the covenant, each reaffirmation of that bond naturally sparked supplications, vows, and gratitude.

2. **National Identity Formed through Joint Prayer** Times of crisis (foreign invasion, famine, plague) pushed the community to gather, fast, and pray. Equally, moments of corporate joy (harvest festivals, Temple dedications) led to jubilant worship. In both extremes—danger or delight—prayer shaped Israel's self-understanding: as a people reliant on God's mercy for survival, yet also chosen to

celebrate His goodness. This cyclical pattern forged a deeper national identity: *We are the people who cry out to God in every season.*

3. **Prophets and Leaders as Catalysts** Often, a leader—be it Moses, Samuel, Elijah, Hezekiah, Ezra, or Nehemiah—would recognize the significance of the moment and call the people to prayer. These individuals functioned as spiritual catalysts, interpreting events (victory, defeat, plague, or prophecy) in the light of God's covenant, urging communal supplication or thanksgiving. Their recognition of God's hand at work shaped collective responses.

4. **Physical Spaces for Sacred Times** The altar, the Tabernacle, the Temple, and later the synagogue provided tangible *locations* that focused the people's awareness on God. While personal prayers could occur anywhere (e.g., Hagar in the wilderness, Daniel in his private room), corporate gatherings often occurred in designated holy spaces, particularly for major feasts or national emergencies. These spaces became *portals in time*, where human crises intersected with divine presence.

5. **Spectrum of Emotions** Moments of prayer in Scripture range from *desperation* (Exodus 14; 2 Chronicles 20) to *elation* (1 Kings 8; Psalm 100). This breadth reaffirms that no human emotion or circumstance lies beyond prayer's scope. Times of transition—like crowning a new king or returning from exile—often blended sorrow for past failures with hope for future blessing, yielding multifaceted prayer gatherings (Nehemiah 8–9).

Chapter 7: Motivations for Prayer (Why Did They Pray)

Prayer, at its core, is an act of communication between finite humans and an infinite, holy God. Yet Scripture reveals that people's reasons for praying are as varied as their life circumstances—ranging from desperation in times of crisis to joyful celebration when blessings flow. Understanding these motivations can provide modern readers not only with historical insight but also with an opportunity for spiritual reflection. How often do we, like the psalmists, pray simply to worship God for who He is, rather than solely seeking what He can do for us? How readily do we follow the example of Old Testament leaders who pleaded for divine guidance in moments of national uncertainty? Or, like New Testament believers, do we feel compelled to intercede for others, trusting that prayer truly makes a difference?

7.1 Seeking God's Will

Many of the prayers in the Bible arise from a desire to *know and follow* God's will. Rather than trusting human instinct alone, biblical figures consistently pause to ask God for clarity, direction, and wisdom. This section focuses on two main aspects of prayer motivated by seeking God's will: **direction for life decisions** and **discernment in times of uncertainty.** Both revolve around acknowledging that God's understanding far surpasses human insight.

7.1.1 Direction for Life Decisions

Acknowledging Divine Sovereignty

Biblical characters often recognized that God, as Creator and Sustainer, has both the wisdom and authority to guide decisions large and small. Their prayers for direction stemmed from an underlying conviction: "God's plan is best." This motivation appears repeatedly in historical narratives and wisdom literature. For instance, the Book of Proverbs encourages seeking God's guidance, as in Proverbs 3:5–6—"Trust in the LORD with all your heart... and he will make straight your paths." Though these verses are not themselves a recorded prayer, they reflect a theological mindset that believers took to heart, prompting them to pray for direction in times of choice.

Examples of Personal Decisions

o **David "Inquires of the LORD"** Before taking military action or relocating his forces, David habitually "inquired of the LORD" (e.g., 1 Samuel 23:1–4; 2 Samuel 2:1). Though earlier chapters have discussed "when" David prayed, the *why* behind these inquiries is crucial: David understood that success depended not on numerical advantage or political alliances but on divine sanction. At each juncture—particularly in 2 Samuel 2:1, where David asks whether he should go up to Hebron to become king—his motivation is to *ensure alignment* with God's will.

- o **Nehemiah's Discreet Petition** When Nehemiah, cupbearer to the Persian King Artaxerxes, hears about Jerusalem's ruined walls, he desires to return and rebuild. His prayer in Nehemiah 1:4–11 includes a plea for success in asking the king's permission. Though we often categorize it as an intercessory or crisis prayer, at its core Nehemiah's motivation is to discover whether God would bless this endeavor. He prays, "Give success to your servant today, and grant him mercy in the sight of this man" (Nehemiah 1:11). Thus, seeking divine direction underpins his confidence to approach earthly authority.

Communal Requests for Guidance

In addition to individual requests, entire communities sought God's will in pivotal decisions:

- **Israel's National Questions** During the period of the Judges, the tribes sometimes gathered to "inquire of the LORD" regarding whether to attack a certain enemy (Judges 20:18, 23, 27–28). Though the outcome was not always straightforward, their motive was clear: *we dare not proceed without confirming God's will.*

- **The Early Church's Decisions** While focusing on Old Testament references can suffice, glancing at one New Testament example affirms the timeless nature of this motive. In Acts 13:2–3, the prophets and teachers in Antioch fast and pray before setting apart Barnabas and Saul for missionary work. Their prayerful worship fosters a collective awareness of the Holy Spirit's guidance—"Set apart for me Barnabas and Saul." Though not a direct focus of earlier chapters, it exemplifies that seeking God's direction transcends historical context, bridging the Old and New Covenants.

Prayers for guidance thus spring from the recognition that human wisdom is finite, but God's perspective is infinite. Whether an Israelite king on the battlefield or a Christian community in a new mission context, the impetus to pray is the same: "Lord, show us the path that aligns with Your will."

7.1.2 Discernment in Times of Uncertainty

Crises of Decision vs. Crises of Faith

Sometimes, biblical figures faced not just everyday decisions but deep uncertainty about *God's overarching plan*. For instance, the prophets often wrestled with doubt when the nation persisted in sin. They sought clarity on how God's justice would unfold or whether mercy was still possible. Such prayers go beyond the immediate "Should I do X or Y?" to the more profound "God, what are You doing in this situation, and how should I respond?"

Habakkuk's Dialogue

The Book of Habakkuk opens with the prophet's complaint: "O LORD, how long shall I cry for help, and you will not hear?" (Habakkuk 1:2). Distressed by rampant injustice in Judah, Habakkuk questions why God tolerates wrongdoing. God's answer—that He will use the Babylonians to judge Judah—provokes further perplexity: *Why use a more wicked nation to punish a less wicked one?* (Habakkuk 1:13). In effect, Habakkuk's entire short book is a prayerful dialogue, culminating in 3:2–19, where he finally confesses trust in God's sovereign ways. This journey underscores that *discernment prayer* can be a long, sometimes anguished process, fueled by a longing to reconcile one's faith in God's goodness with the grim realities of life.

Daniel's Prophetic Insight

Similarly, Daniel 9 is motivated by Daniel discovering Jeremiah's prophecy of seventy years for Jerusalem's desolation. The immediate question: *Now that seventy years approach completion, does restoration loom near?* Daniel's prayer includes confession, but the underlying motive is to discern how God's timeline aligns with present circumstances. Daniel pleads, "O Lord, hear! O Lord, forgive! O Lord, pay attention and act!" (Daniel 9:19). God responds through the angel Gabriel, providing a broader vision that extends beyond Daniel's immediate concerns. This illustrates how seeking clarity in uncertain times sometimes results in revelations that surpass even the original question.

Personal Uncertainties: Job's Wrestlings

Though the Book of Job is largely a poetic dialogue with Job's friends, interspersed are Job's addresses to God—raw, unfiltered pleas to understand *why* he suffers innocently (Job 13:20–24; 31:35–37). His repeated refrain, "Let the Almighty answer me!" underscores a longing for discernment. Job's unwavering trust that God holds the answers, even if hidden for a season, underscores this motive. While we do not find a neat resolution until God speaks in Job 38–42, the impetus behind Job's prayers is stark: in the face of inexplicable suffering, he yearns for clarity and vindication from the only One who can provide it.

Whether grappling with personal suffering, societal injustice, or uncertain futures, biblical believers recognized that God alone possessed the ultimate viewpoint. Seeking that viewpoint—*Why is this happening? How should we proceed?*—stands as a core motivation for prayer in times of deep uncertainty.

7.2 Expressing Worship and Gratitude

Prayer is not merely about asking. Some of Scripture's most beautiful prayers are *pure expressions of adoration* for God's character or *simple thanksgivings* for blessings received. This section discusses how praise and gratitude emerge as central motivations for prayer, revealing a side of communication with God that is not transactional but relational and reverential.

7.2.1 Thanking God for His Provision

Biblical Emphasis on Thanksgiving

From the earliest narratives, worshipers lifted prayers of gratitude. After the flood, Noah built an altar (Genesis 8:20) to honor God's deliverance. While this act involves sacrifice, it also frames an implicit prayer of thanks—Noah's recognition that he, his family, and the creatures with him have been preserved from global disaster. In the broader sweep of Scripture, thanksgiving often goes hand in hand with acknowledging God's gracious acts.

Examples of Individual Gratitude

- o **Hannah's Song** (1 Samuel 2:1–10) After God answers her earnest plea for a child, Hannah responds not with a mere "thank you," but with an exuberant hymn praising God's sovereignty and reversing of fortunes. She proclaims, "My heart exults in the LORD... There is none holy like the LORD" (vv. 1–2). The impetus is gratitude—"I prayed for this child, and God granted my request"—yet Hannah's thanks flows into declarations of God's cosmic rule, thus linking personal blessing with broader theological affirmations.

- o **Mary's Magnificat** (Luke 1:46–55) Though a New

Testament parallel, Mary's response to the Annunciation mirrors Hannah's. Pregnant with the Messiah, she exclaims, "My soul magnifies the Lord, and my spirit rejoices in God my Savior" (Luke 1:46–47). Mary's gratitude for God's favor leads her to praise His power, holiness, and mercy. This link between *personal experience* (bearing Christ) and *universal truths* (God's faithfulness to Israel) is a hallmark of biblical thanksgiving prayers.

Communal Acts of Thanksgiving

- **Israel's Festivals** Feasts like the Feast of Harvest (Pentecost) and the Feast of Booths (Tabernacles) inherently centered on thankfulness for God's provision, especially the yearly harvest (Deuteronomy 16:9–17). Though earlier chapters addressed *when* such feasts occurred, the *why* is vital here: the festival prayers highlight that Israel recognized each harvest, each new season, as an occasion to express collective gratitude.

- **Psalms of Thanksgiving** Many of the psalms, labeled "psalms of thanksgiving," reflect corporate motivations. For example, Psalm 100:4 urges believers to "enter his gates with thanksgiving, and his courts with praise," instructing worshipers to come before God *motivated* by grateful hearts. The impetus is not crisis or petition but the desire to celebrate God's blessings and character within the Temple setting.

Overall, gratitude-based prayer underscores that one key motivation is not what we *lack* but what we *already have* in God. By turning blessings into thanks, believers perpetuate a cycle of recognizing God's generosity and fostering deeper worship.

7.2.2 Magnifying the Character of God

Praise as an End in Itself

In numerous biblical prayers, the driving force is *simply to exalt God for who He is*. This impetus differs from prayers for help or guidance, as the worshiper's primary focus is on God's attributes— His holiness, love, power, justice, and faithfulness. Such doxological prayers appear in both Old and New Testaments:

- **Isaiah's Vision** (Isaiah 6:1–5) Isaiah's vision in the Temple includes angelic beings crying, "Holy, holy, holy is the LORD of hosts; the whole earth is full of his glory!" Although not framed as a prayer from Isaiah, the prophet's reaction— "Woe is me!"—connects to the recognition of God's holiness. Motivated by awe, Isaiah's immediate stance is that of reverent submission. Such moments remind us that encountering God's presence can lead to prayer that is pure adoration, devoid of request but laden with reverence.

- **Revelation's Heavenly Scenes** (Revelation 4:8–11; 5:8–14) In John's apocalyptic vision, heavenly creatures and elders perpetually offer worship to the enthroned Lord and to the Lamb. Their repeated acclamations ("Worthy are you, our Lord and God…!") reveal a prime motive: to declare God's worthiness. Although set in a future or transcendent realm, these examples provide a pattern for earthly prayer as well. The impetus is to magnify God's character, praising the Creator's majesty and the Redeemer's sacrifice.

Expressions of Honor and Devotion

Prayers of praise often take the form of exalting God's name, recounting His mighty works, or extolling His covenant faithfulness. When David brings the ark to Jerusalem (1 Chronicles 15–16), he composes a psalm praising God's deeds and urging the people to "tell of all his wondrous works!" (1 Chronicles 16:9). The entire ceremony is a testament that the *why* behind communal prayer includes lifting God's name high.

Transformative Power of Worshipful Prayer

When believers pray primarily to honor God's character, the act itself can reshape perspectives. Instead of focusing on personal circumstances—good or bad—the worshipper gazes upon God's transcendence. This often leads to a deeper sense of trust, humility, and peace because magnifying God's greatness implicitly reminds the worshipper of God's ability to sustain and govern the universe. Thus, while the impetus is *God-centered rather than need-centered*, it still yields spiritual benefits for the one who prays.

7.3 Confession and Repentance

Few motivations are more evident in Scripture than the impetus to confess sin and seek divine mercy. Whether at an individual or corporate level, confession-based prayers reveal that the recognition of wrongdoing can drive one to the feet of a holy God, pleading for forgiveness and restoration. This section covers both **personal sin and atonement** and **corporate or national repentance** as key facets of prayer's motivations.

7.3.1 Personal Sin and Atonement

Understanding the Need for Atonement

Within Israel's sacrificial system, the process of atonement for sin involved offerings and the mediation of priests (see Leviticus 1–7). However, the outward ritual often coincided with heartfelt prayer. In King David's life, this connection emerges powerfully: after his adultery with Bathsheba and the subsequent rebuke by Nathan,

David pens Psalm 51. The driving force behind his lament? A need for personal cleansing: "Wash me thoroughly from my iniquity, and cleanse me from my sin!" (Psalm 51:2). David's awareness of his transgression against God compels him to pray, acknowledging, "Against you, you only, have I sinned" (Psalm 51:4). The impetus here is deeply relational: David craves restored fellowship with God, which sin has marred.

Examples of Individual Confessions

o **Ezra's Personal Identification** (Ezra 9:5–15) Though this prayer also represents corporate guilt (discussed below), Ezra's posture demonstrates personal contrition. He tears his clothes and falls on his knees, stating, "O my God, I am ashamed... to lift my face to you" (Ezra 9:6). Even though much of the wrongdoing—intermarriage with pagan nations—predated or surpassed his direct involvement, Ezra includes himself in the shame. The impetus is a deeply felt sorrow for sin and a resolve to confess in the hope of mercy.

o **Job's Final Submission** (Job 42:1–6) After God's speeches in Job 38–41, Job repents "in dust and ashes" (42:6). While Job's earlier pleas revolve around vindication, the culminating moment is one of humbling himself before God's greatness. Although Job was not guilty of the sins his friends accused him of, his final stance is still that of confession—acknowledging finite understanding and possible pride in challenging God's justice. Thus, the impetus for prayer is an awakened realization of his limited perspective, prompting contrition.

At-One-Ment Through Confession

Confessional prayer in Scripture demonstrates that the worshiper's aim is not merely to *admit* wrongdoing but to *reconcile* with God—what older English texts call "atonement" (at-one-ment). The impetus is bridging the gulf sin creates. Psalm 32 captures this dynamic: David describes the burden of unconfessed sin and the relief that comes after acknowledging it to the Lord. Thus, personal confession-based prayer is driven by the desire for renewed intimacy and peace with God.

7.3.2 Corporate or National Repentance

Collective Realization of Guilt

Entire communities sometimes recognized that they had strayed from divine commandments, prompting large-scale acts of public contrition. This was not a superficial ritual but a profoundly motivated approach to re-align the nation or community with God's covenant.

- **Samuel at Mizpah** (1 Samuel 7:6) As recounted in earlier chapters, the people fasted and admitted, "We have sinned against the LORD." Although we have previously noted *when* this occurred (during Philistine threats), the deeper motive is confession. The crisis revealed their spiritual drift, so the impetus for prayer was *to restore covenant alignment* with God.

- **Nehemiah 9** The returned exiles publicly read the Law and engaged in a prolonged confession of their historical sins (Nehemiah 9:1–3). Rather than focusing solely on personal wrongdoing, the prayer references ancestors' rebellions, signifying the entire lineage's guilt. The impetus is a dual recognition: (1) God's unwavering faithfulness through generations, (2) the people's repeated pattern of rebellion.

The prayer thus becomes a collective turning point—a motivation to secure God's mercy for the present and future.

The Role of Leadership in Corporate Confession

Leaders often catalyze corporate repentance:

- **Josiah's Reforms** (2 Kings 22–23) After discovering the Book of the Law, King Josiah tears his clothes in despair, realizing Judah's rampant disobedience. He leads the nation in renewing the covenant, demolishing idols, and restoring correct worship. Though the text focuses more on actions than recorded prayers, it is clear Josiah's impetus is *national repentance*, sparked by rediscovered Scripture.

- **Joel's Call for Solemn Assembly** (Joel 2:12–17) The prophet Joel instructs the priests, elders, and all inhabitants to gather, fast, and cry out to God in the face of a locust plague. Joel's motivational cry—"Return to me with all your heart"—conveys that the crisis is not merely agricultural but spiritual. The impetus for communal prayer is an urgent recognition that God alone can restore them if they wholeheartedly repent.

Outcome of Corporate Confessional Prayer

Often, Scripture illustrates that God responds favorably when the people collectively humble themselves. 2 Chronicles 7:14 famously states, "If my people who are called by my name humble themselves, and pray and seek my face and turn from their wicked ways, then I will hear… and heal their land." While the immediate context is Solomon's dedication of the Temple, the principle underscores that *repentance-based prayer* can shift a nation's destiny, reflecting God's readiness to forgive when people sincerely turn from their sins.

Thus, whether personal or collective, confession and repentance consistently emerge as driving motivations in biblical prayer. The impetus is spiritual restoration, bridging the gap between a holy God and a people conscious of their failings.

7.4 Intercession and Petition

Perhaps the most commonly assumed motivation for prayer is to *ask God for something*, whether on one's own behalf (petition) or on behalf of others (intercession). Scripture presents a vast array of such requests, spanning mundane needs and miraculous deliverances. This section breaks it down into **advocating for others** and **pleading for healing and deliverance**, though the categories often intersect.

7.4.1 Advocating for Others

Biblical Foundations for Intercession

From early on, figures like Abraham interceded for entire cities (Genesis 18:22–33), and Moses repeatedly petitioned for God to spare Israel despite their sins (Exodus 32:11–14, Numbers 14:13–20). Their prayers illustrate a selfless motivation: *pleading for mercy or blessing on someone else's behalf.* Jesus, too, models intercession in the New Testament (John 17), praying for His disciples and all future believers.

Patterns of Intercession

- o **Standing in the Gap** Ezekiel 22:30 laments that God sought someone "to stand in the gap" for the land but found none. The imagery evokes a breach in the city wall: the intercessor places themselves in that breach, shielding the people from God's judgment. The impetus behind such prayer is compassion—seeing others in peril or sin and yearning for their rescue.

- o **Priestly Role** In the Old Covenant, priests were literal mediators between God and Israel, offering sacrifices and prayers. Aaron's responsibility included atoning for the people's sin (Leviticus 16). This underscores that intercession can be an official role, yet Scripture also portrays laypersons stepping into that function (e.g., Hannah praying for a child, who would bless the nation). By extension, the New Testament calls all believers a "royal priesthood" (1 Peter 2:9), suggesting that *every* Christian shares in intercessory privilege and responsibility.

New Testament Examples

While the Old Testament provides abundant intercessory models, the New Testament cements it as a core part of Christian life:

- **Epistolary Prayers**: Paul's letters brim with intercessory content, as he prays "unceasingly" for the churches (Philippians 1:3–4; Colossians 1:9; 1 Thessalonians 1:2). His motivation is spiritual growth for believers—"that you may be filled with the knowledge of his will" (Colossians 1:9).

- **Wider Church Intercession**: Acts 12:5 shows the Jerusalem church praying fervently for Peter's release from prison. The impetus is clear: love for a fellow apostle, concern for the gospel's advance, and belief that God can intervene. Intercession, then, emerges as an expression of unity and mutual care within the body of Christ.

Thus, advocating for others—whether seeking forgiveness for their sins, deliverance from danger, or spiritual edification—remains a potent biblical motive for prayer. It flows from empathy, shared covenant identity, and trust in God's mercy.

7.4.2 Pleading for Healing and Deliverance

Physical Healing

Scripture is replete with instances of individuals beseeching God for bodily healing or approaching prophets and Jesus Himself with requests for miraculous interventions:

- **King Hezekiah's Illness** (Isaiah 38; 2 Kings 20:1–11) When the prophet Isaiah informs Hezekiah that he will die, the king turns his face to the wall and prays, weeping bitterly. God responds by adding fifteen years to his life, providing a sign (the sun's shadow moving backward). Hezekiah's impetus is immediate personal survival, but the prayer also underscores that God is intimately concerned with the believer's physical needs.

- **The Gospels' Miracle Accounts** Many who approached Jesus—lepers (Matthew 8:2), the centurion for his servant (Matthew 8:5–13), Jairus for his daughter (Mark 5:22–24, 35–43)—were motivated by dire medical or life-threatening circumstances. Their pleas exemplify petition. The impetus is unvarnished desperation, often fused with faith in Jesus's power. While these narratives revolve around Jesus's direct presence, they mirror the same underlying motive found in Old Testament prayers for healing or longevity.

Spiritual and Demonic Deliverance

Alongside physical healing, Scripture abounds with requests for spiritual rescue:

- **Demoniacs Seeking Freedom** Those possessed or oppressed by evil spirits—like the boy in Mark 9:17–29—relied on Jesus's authority. Though not always framed as "prayers," the pleas from the father ("I believe; help my unbelief!") show that the impetus is to see the captive released.

- **Protection from Enemies or Dark Forces** Beyond demon possession, believers prayed for protection from satanic schemes or oppressive powers. Psalm 91 stands out as a poetic expression of trust in God's deliverance from deadly pestilence, snares, and hidden terrors. While it does not depict an explicit prayer by a biblical character, its content implies a motivation to cling to God's safeguarding presence, particularly in spiritual or unseen conflicts.

Broader Spectrum of "Deliverance"

"Deliverance" in Scripture can encompass rescue from famine, financial distress, or any dire situation. Ruth's entire story underscores how Naomi, bitter and bereft, eventually sees God's providential deliverance through Boaz. Although not every cry is explicitly labeled a prayer, the impetus for gleaners and widows to turn to God is clear: "Without Your help, we have no future." Biblical petition thus extends beyond the purely spiritual to the ordinary, physical aspects of life, confirming that *nothing is too mundane* or too grand to bring before God.

7.5 Extended Reflections on Motivations for Prayer

Having examined four major categories—seeking God's will, expressing worship and gratitude, confessing sin, and interceding or petitioning for needs—several overarching reflections emerge:

Relational Depth Beyond Transaction

Biblical prayer is more than a transaction: "I need something; God can provide." In multiple examples (such as Mary's Magnificat or the seraphic cries of Isaiah 6), prayer emerges from adoration, delight, and awe. Even requests for help, if approached biblically, often stem from recognizing who God is—faithful, holy, and loving—rather than merely from a desire to secure benefits. This relational dimension shapes how we interpret "why they prayed": it wasn't just about results but about *restoring, sustaining, or deepening communion* with God.

Diverse Motivations, One Divine Source

Though motivations differ—one day for forgiveness, another day for harvest thanksgiving—each impetus acknowledges God as the ultimate source. People prayed for physical healing because they trusted God could intervene; they prayed to confess sin because they believed He had the authority to forgive and restore. They worshiped Him because they recognized He alone deserved glory. In all cases, the underlying theology is that God is sovereign, able, and worthy to be approached.

Covenantal Framework

Especially in the Old Testament, many motivations arise from Israel's covenant relationship with Yahweh. They confess sin because they have violated covenant terms. They give thanks for harvest because they see it as covenant blessing (Deuteronomy 28). They intercede for rebellious kin because they want God's covenant mercies to endure. This covenantal lens remains relevant in the New Testament, where believers pray as adopted children of God in Christ, trusting in the "new covenant" sealed by Jesus's blood (Luke 22:20; Hebrews 8–9).

Communal vs. Individual Motivations

A single impetus can manifest differently at the personal or communal level. For instance, *confession* might be an individual's private cry (Psalm 51) or a nationwide lament (Nehemiah 9). *Seeking God's will* might guide an individual (David) or a congregation (Acts 13). *Thanksgiving* might be personal (Hannah) or corporate (the entire assembly at the Temple dedication). Each scenario underscores that the reasons for prayer do not remain locked within personal devotion; they ripple into shared spiritual life.

Biblical Honesty: Joy and Sorrow Alike

A final reflection is the Bible's raw authenticity: motivations for prayer can be joyful, anguished, repentant, or hopeful. This breadth signals that God welcomes every human emotion and need, from the ecstasy of victory to the depths of despair. Far from a monolithic act, prayer in the Bible is richly varied because life itself is multifaceted. Each motive leads back to the same truth: God is near and responsive to those who seek Him.

Chapter 8: Purity in Prayer (What Prayer Should Not Be)

Prayer in Scripture is both a privilege and a responsibility. While God warmly invites us into fellowship, He also commands sincerity, humility, and faith. The numerous warnings about *wrong motives* or *hypocritical attitudes* underscore that not every utterance labeled "prayer" pleases the Lord. From Old Testament prophets condemning ritualistic show to Jesus's critique of ostentatious Pharisees, the Bible consistently reveals that a corrupt heart can render the holiest-sounding prayers abominable.

8.1 Vain Repetition and Empty Words

Prayer can quickly degenerate into meaningless chatter when the worshipper places more emphasis on formulaic or repetitive expressions than on heartfelt devotion. Jesus specifically warned His followers about "empty phrases" (Matthew 6:7), and the Old Testament also contains rebukes for thoughtless religious speech. In this section, we delve into:

- What constitutes "vain repetition" or empty words,

- Why does Scripture denounce such patterns, and

- Examples of how believers can cultivate thoughtful sincerity rather than rote incantations.

8.1.1 The Warning Against Babbling

Jesus's Teaching in the Sermon on the Mount

In Matthew 6:7, Jesus says, "And when you pray, do not heap up empty phrases as the Gentiles do, for they think that they will be heard for their many words." The Greek term, often translated as "empty phrases" or "vain repetitions" (battalogeo), suggests meaningless babble or mechanical repetition of words. Jesus contrasts this with the principle that *God already knows what we need* (Matthew 6:8). The impetus behind prayer is not to manipulate or impress the Lord through sheer verbosity, but to commune with Him sincerely.

Cultural Context

Jesus's reference to "the Gentiles" likely alludes to pagan practices where worshipers repeated incantations or formulas in attempts to elicit favor from their gods. In some ancient religions, lengthy recitations were believed to coerce a deity or align cosmic forces. By contrast, biblical prayer is fundamentally relational—an expression of faith in a loving, sovereign God who cares for His people. When we reduce prayer to repetitious mantras or mindless incantations, we depart from the biblical ethos of personal, engaged communion with the Father.

Misconceptions About Quantity Over Quality

The problem Jesus addresses is not the *length* of prayers per se. Scripture records extended prayers (e.g., Nehemiah 9 or John 17) that are heartfelt and profound. Rather, the emphasis lies on the quality of engagement over sheer word count. A prayer can be lengthy yet deeply sincere or short yet powerful (e.g., "Lord, save me!" in Matthew 14:30). In vain repetition, the worshipper presumes that the deity can be swayed by many words, forgetting that God values genuine contrition, reverence, and trust.

8.1.2 Heartless Ritual vs. Sincere Relationship

Old Testament Rebukes of Empty Formalism

The prophets frequently denounce Israel's reliance on outward ritual devoid of inward devotion. Isaiah 29:13 laments, "this people draw near with their mouth… while their hearts are far from me." Though not always explicitly about prayer, this rebuke parallels Jesus's teaching: outward piety—words spoken, sacrifices offered—cannot mask a heart that lacks true reverence. A purely mechanical repetition of religious phrases or repeated formulas rings hollow to God (Isaiah 1:11–15).

Hannah's Contrasting Example

While Scripture condemns babbling, it celebrates *sincere* outpourings—even silent ones. Hannah's prayer in 1 Samuel 1:10–16 was so intense that her lips moved without audible words, prompting Eli to think she was drunk. This prayer exemplifies the opposite of vain repetition: deeply personal, heartfelt, and unafraid to bare genuine emotions before God. Though her words were not repeated incantations, they carried potent authenticity. *Purity of prayer rests in sincerity, not formulaic precision.*

Practical Guardrails

How can modern believers avoid drifting into vain repetition or empty words?

- **Mindful Focus**: Before speaking, pause to recollect God's presence and direct your heart toward Him.

- **Intentional Variety**: If using set prayers or liturgies, vary expression or reflect deeply on each phrase. Tradition can be valuable—but only when engaged with understanding and conviction, not mechanical recitation.

- **Simplicity and Honesty**: Jesus's model prayer (Matthew 6:9–13) is brief yet profound. Sincere brevity, free from showy verbiage, often aligns well with humble dependence on God.

8.1.3 Avoiding Flippant or Superficial Requests

Finally, the concept of "empty words" extends beyond repetitive babbling to superficial or thoughtless requests. When believers treat prayer as casual filler—"Lord, just bless everything" with no real engagement—they risk trivializing communion with God. This does not mean we cannot pray briefly; rather, we must be mindful and genuine, remembering that prayer is sacred conversation with the Lord of heaven and earth.

8.2 Self-Centered Requests

Another distortion of prayer arises when the worshiper's primary or exclusive focus is *personal gain*, disregarding God's will or the well-being of others. While Scripture permits believers to present their needs, it also repeatedly warns against prayers driven by selfish ambition, greed, or purely material desires. In this section, we explore:

- The biblical condemnation of self-indulgent motives,

- How prayers can become self-centered,

- Practical ways to align our requests with God's purposes.

8.2.1 Pure Motives vs. Personal Gain

James's Indictment of Wrong Motives

In James 4:3, the apostle confronts believers: "You ask and do not receive, because you ask wrongly, to spend it on your passions." Here, the phrase "ask wrongly" (kakos in Greek) implies moral deficiency in motivation. James clarifies that such requests revolve around gratifying one's own lusts or indulgences. Prayer intended solely for self-gratification misrepresents the heart of biblical devotion, which aims at God's glory and kingdom priorities (Matthew 6:33).

Old Testament Cautions

While James provides a direct statement, the Old Testament also highlights the folly of self-serving pleas. For instance, consider Balaam's contradictory stance in Numbers 22–24. Though not a straightforward prayer narrative, Balaam attempts to "inquire of the LORD" yet harbors greed for Balak's reward. His partial compliance and ultimate disregard for Israel's welfare (Numbers 31:16) reflect how a desire for personal profit can corrupt one's spiritual posture. Although Balaam does not utter a typical prayer to bless or curse Israel for personal gain (he somewhat does—he's paid to curse), the broader scenario underscores that *seeking to harness divine power for self-interest is antithetical to genuine faith*.

Contrast with Selfless Intercessions

Throughout Scripture, righteous figures pray for others or for God's will, not merely themselves. Moses pleads for Israel's forgiveness (Exodus 32:11–14), Daniel prays for the exiled community (Daniel 9:3–19), and Paul intercedes for the churches (Philippians 1:3–11). Their examples stand in stark contrast to those who approach God solely to accumulate personal pleasures or accolades.

8.2.2 The Danger of Pride in Prayer

Boasting in Spiritual Achievement

Self-centered prayers can also manifest as prideful boasting—relating to God primarily to flaunt one's piety or spiritual accomplishments. Jesus's parable of the Pharisee and the tax collector (Luke 18:9–14) vividly portrays a Pharisee who "prayed thus with himself," essentially reciting his virtues (fasting, tithing) while scorning others. Though this parable often highlights hypocrisy and self-righteousness, it equally underscores that a prayer saturated with *self* rather than *God* defies the humility essential to true communion.

Nebuchadnezzar's Hubris

In Daniel 4:29–37, King Nebuchadnezzar exults in the grandeur of Babylon as if it were his own creation. Though not framed as a direct prayer, his boastful words illustrate the mindset of attributing success solely to oneself. God swiftly humbles him, driving him to live like a beast until he acknowledges divine sovereignty. This narrative, while not a typical prayer scene, parallels the principle that self-exaltation is incompatible with genuine prayer, which must revere God's supremacy over all human achievements.

The Need for Christlike Humility

To avoid self-centered or prideful prayers, believers must cultivate humility, echoing Jesus's posture in Gethsemane: "Not my will, but yours, be done" (Luke 22:42). This stance dethrones self-interest, reorienting requests around God's plan and the broader good of others. A humble heart stands open to God's correction, aware that every blessing—material or spiritual—flows from grace rather than merit.

8.2.3 Balancing Personal Needs with Kingdom Focus

Scripture does not forbid praying for personal needs; on the contrary, Jesus taught us to petition for "daily bread" (Matthew 6:11). The key difference is *motivation*. Self-centered prayers treat God as a means to personal ends, ignoring His kingdom and glory. Faithful prayer, conversely, nestles personal requests within a larger submission to God's authority: "Your kingdom come, your will be done" (Matthew 6:10). By seeking alignment with divine purposes, believers ensure their petitions remain pure, free from greed or vainglory.

8.3 Legalistic or Showy Prayers

A third corrupting influence arises when prayer becomes a public performance or a legalistic obligation rather than an authentic encounter with God. This section unpacks the pitfalls of prayer aimed at impressing others, following rigid rituals for its own sake, or manipulating God through external forms. We explore:

- Jesus's criticism of ostentatious prayers,

- Old Testament parallels condemning hollow formalism,

- The difference between communal worship and showy public displays.

8.3.1 The Pharisees' Example of Public Performance

Jesus's Explicit Condemnation

In Matthew 6:5, Jesus warns, "When you pray, you must not be like the hypocrites. For they love to stand and pray in the synagogues and at the street corners, that they may be seen by others." The key phrase "that they may be seen" highlights the fundamental flaw: prayer is misused as a stage for self-promotion. The very act that should direct honor to God is co-opted for human applause.

Social and Religious Context

First-century Judea was a deeply religious society where public piety often garnered respect. The Pharisees, admired for their strict observance of the Law, could slip into the temptation of turning prayer into a spectacle. Jesus clarifies that they have already received their "reward" (human admiration), implying no further blessing from God. Contrastingly, He prescribes private communion—"go into your room and shut the door and pray to your Father who is in secret" (Matthew 6:6)—emphasizing sincerity over performance.

Showy Prayer in the Modern Context

While we may not typically stand on street corners, the principle remains pertinent. Believers can still fall into subtle forms of showy prayer—e.g., using flowery language in group settings to impress peers, boasting of extended prayer sessions on social media, or choreographing public devotion to gain popularity. The question is: *Am I praying to God, or performing for an audience?*

8.3.2 Cultivating Genuine Devotion

Ritual vs. Heart Engagement

Ritual prayers—whether daily offices, liturgies, or set times—are not inherently problematic. Indeed, the psalmists followed structured patterns (e.g., morning and evening sacrifices). The issue arises when the ritual becomes an end in itself, *divorced from heartfelt devotion.* Isaiah 1:13–15 underscores God's disgust at Israel's "meaningless offerings" and "solemn assemblies" performed without genuine repentance. *When the heart is absent, religious form becomes legalistic and hollow.*

Jesus's Private Prayer Life

Luke frequently shows Jesus retreating alone to pray (Luke 5:16; 6:12). This underscores that prayer, though it can be communal, must be grounded in authentic, personal connection with the Father. Even when Jesus prays publicly—e.g., giving thanks before feeding the 5,000 (Matthew 14:19)—His aim is to honor the Father, not garner human accolades. This balanced example endorses corporate worship while cautioning against superficial pageantry.

Guidelines for Corporate Prayer

Corporate prayer is biblical and vital (Acts 2:42; 4:24–31). Avoiding showy or legalistic prayers does not mean believers should shun public gatherings. Instead, the heart posture should be:

- **Unity**: Praying as one body, seeking God's glory and communal edification, not individual display.

- **Clarity and Simplicity**: Ensuring words serve to uplift and unify rather than become a platform for eloquent self-promotion.

- **Focus on God**: Corporate prayers should revolve around praising God, confessing sin, and interceding for kingdom concerns, not highlighting personal virtue or achievements.

8.3.3 Freed from Bondage to Appearances

When prayer is contaminated by legalism or performance, it enslaves worshipers to the opinions of others. Instead of resting in God's acceptance, the person must maintain a facade of piety. Jesus's teaching liberates us from this tyranny. True prayer thrives in authenticity—approaching God in reverent fear, sincere love, and unfeigned humility. When we realize we do not have to prove ourselves before men, we enter the blessed freedom of intimacy with our Father, who sees us in secret.

8.4 Insincere Confessions

The final section we explore in this book concerns prayers of confession that lack genuine repentance or contrition. Confession is a key biblical practice (as seen in Chapter 7 on motivations for prayer), but Scripture also shows how such prayers can be insincere—mere lip service that does not reflect a changed heart. In this section, we investigate:

- The difference between outward confession and true contrition,

- Biblical examples of half-hearted or hypocritical repentance,

- How to ensure authenticity in confessing sin before God.

8.4.1 Lip Service vs. True Repentance

The Prophet Isaiah's Indictment

Isaiah 58 addresses a scenario where Israel fasts and outwardly humbles themselves, yet continues to oppress the poor and engage in strife (Isaiah 58:2–4). They appear pious—fasting, praying, wearing sackcloth—while their hearts remain callous. God rejects such displays, stating that the fast He desires is justice, mercy, and genuine transformation (Isaiah 58:6–7). Although the passage primarily discusses fasting, the principle extends to confession prayer: *words of repentance are empty if they do not flow from a penitent heart committed to obedience.*

King Saul's Hollow "Confession"

In 1 Samuel 15, King Saul disobeys God's command to destroy Amalek's spoils. When the prophet Samuel confronts him, Saul initially blames the people. Then, under pressure, he declares, "I have sinned... because I feared the people" (1 Samuel 15:24). Yet his subsequent behavior—asking Samuel to honor him before the elders (v. 30)—reveals a deeper concern for saving face than for aligning with God's will. His confession lacks genuine sorrow over wrongdoing, serving more as damage control than spiritual contrition. This incident highlights that superficial words of remorse do not fool God nor rectify the rift that sin causes.

3.   **Contrast with David's Penitence**

By comparing Saul's response with David's heartfelt confession in Psalm 51, we see a stark difference. David exclaims, "Against you, you only, have I sinned" (v. 4), and pleads for a clean heart (v. 10). While both men utter words of acknowledgment, David's humility and longing for restored fellowship demonstrate sincerity. True confession emerges from a broken and contrite spirit (Psalm 51:17), whereas false confession is purely external, seeking to placate God or others without real moral transformation.

8.4.2 Harboring Sin While Praying

1.   **Jeremiah's Rebuke of Hypocrisy**

Jeremiah laments that Israel's leaders cry "Peace, peace" when there is no peace (Jeremiah 6:14). This broader hypocrisy also taints their worship, including prayer. People bring sacrifices or recite confessions while persisting in idolatry and oppression. They effectively want the benefits of God's favor without forsaking sin. The "double-minded man" James speaks of (James 1:8) exemplifies this dynamic: attempting to serve two masters, inwardly clinging to unrighteousness while outwardly appearing devout.

2.   **Jesus's Words on Forgiveness**

In Mark 11:25, Jesus instructs that when we stand praying, we must forgive others if we have anything against them so that the Father may forgive us. Prayers of confession ring hollow if we ourselves refuse to forgive or cling to bitterness. By harboring resentments, we undermine the sincerity of our own repentance. The impetus for confession is a restored relationship with God, which extends horizontally to reconciled relationships with others (1 John 4:20).

3.   **Resolution Through Genuine Repentance**

True repentance entails not only confessing sin but also turning away from it. A prayer that repeatedly confesses the same wrongdoing without any intention or effort to change verges on insincerity. While growth in holiness is a lifelong process, the contrite heart actively seeks the Spirit's empowerment to overcome sin. Authentic confession is accompanied by a commitment—however imperfect—to live differently, trusting God's grace to effect real transformation.

8.4.3 Indicators of Authentic Confession

How can believers ensure their confession prayers reflect genuine contrition rather than empty lip service? A few biblical markers:

- **Brokenness Over Sin**: Does the heart grieve the offense committed against God's holiness (Psalm 51:4)?

- **Desire for Change**: Is there a conscious resolve to forsake sin, or is the prayer simply a ritual formula for absolution?

- **Openness to Accountability**: Authentic repentance often involves restitution or seeking accountability from mature believers, if appropriate (Luke 19:8).

- **Focus on God's Character**: True confession extols God's mercy and justice, humbly receiving His forgiveness rather than presuming upon it.

8.5 Extended Reflections on "What Prayer Should Not Be"

Having identified four major pitfalls—vain repetition, self-centered

requests, showy or legalistic prayers, and insincere confessions—
we can draw overarching insights about maintaining purity in
prayer:

1. God Sees the Heart

Central to each cautionary scenario is the fact that outward
appearances can deceive human observers but never God. He
discerns genuine humility from disguised arrogance, sincerity from
rote formalism. This biblical perspective fosters a reverential awe:
we pray before the One who knows our deepest motivations. Rather
than inciting fear, this truth should spur us to pray with
authenticity, trusting that God graciously welcomes honest hearts
(Hebrews 4:16).

2. Prayer is Primarily Relational, Not Transactional

When prayers become manipulative—attempting to coerce God via
repetition or flaunting piety before others—they shift from a
relational posture to a transactional one. But Scripture insists that
prayer is the child speaking to the Father, the servant appealing to
the King, or the friend confiding in the Savior. Reducing prayer to a
formula, performance, or self-promotion betrays its divine-human
relational core.

3. Holistic Integrity is Required

Biblical prayer never stands alone as a mere religious act; it
intertwines with the worshiper's entire life. As Jesus repeatedly
taught, incongruence between one's daily conduct and one's
prayerful words is hypocrisy. Purity in prayer demands an
integrated life, where the same devotion offered in private
communion shapes public ethics and relationships. The prophets
hammered this point: if you oppress the vulnerable or worship
idols, your prayers ring hollow (Isaiah 1:15–17; Amos 5:21–24).

4.   **Repeated Warnings Suggest Common Human Struggles**

The frequency of these admonitions in Scripture implies that believers in every era face these temptations. Indeed, biblical prayer is not for super-saints immune to sin; it is for real people grappling with pride, distraction, or hypocrisy. Knowing how easy it is to lapse into vain repetition, self-centeredness, or legalism, wise believers constantly examine their hearts, seeking the Holy Spirit's guidance to maintain purity.

5.   **Grace Overweighs Our Shortcomings**

Despite these strong warnings, Scripture consistently emphasizes that God desires genuine connection more than flawless performance. Even those who have stumbled into hypocrisy or selfish motives can repent and restore sincerity in prayer. The same God who rebukes insincere worship is the One who promises, "Return to me… and I will return to you" (Zechariah 1:3). He delights in receiving honest pleas for help in realigning our hearts with His.

www.ingramcontent.com/pod-product-compliance
Lightning Source LLC
Chambersburg PA
CBHW060325050426
42449CB00011B/2661